Being Human

Being Human

Diagnosis in Curative Education

Karl König, M.D.

Translated by Catherine Creeger

Anthroposophic Press

This book is a translation of the two booklets *Heilpädagogische Diagnostik* (1983), prepared for publication by Dr. Georg von Arnim, and *Epilepsie und Hysterie* (1984). They were published in German by Natura Verlag in Arlesheim, Switzerland. This first translation into English of these booklets was made with the kind permission of Natura Verlag.

Published in the United States of America by Anthroposophic Press, R. R. 4, Box 94A, Hudson, New York 12534.

Published in the United Kingdom by Camphill Press, Danby, Whitby, N. Yorkshire Y021 2NJ.

© Copyright 1989 by Anthroposophic Press, Inc., and Camphill Press

Library of Congress Cataloging-in-Publication Data

König, Karl, 1902–1966.
 [Heilpädagogische Diagnostik. English]
 Being human: diagnosis in curative education / Karl König; translated by Catherine Creeger.
 p. cm.
 Translation of: Heilpädagogische Diagnostik, and, Epilepsie und Hysterie.
 Includes bibliographical references.
 ISBN 0-88010-280-2 AP
 ISBN 0-904145-38-7 CP
 1. Mental illness. 2. Child development. 3. Epilepsy. 4. Hysteria. I. König, Karl, 1902–1966. Epilepsie und Hysterie. English. II. Title.
 RC458.K6313   1989
 618.92'89'001—dc20   89-18086
                                                                           CIP

All rights reserved. No part of this book may be reproduced in any form without the written permission of the publishers, except for brief quotations embodied in critical articles and reviews.

Printed in the United States of America

Contents

Foreword
by Dr. Michaela Glöckler, M.D vii

Introduction
by Cornelius Pietzner..ix

PART I

THE ANTHROPOLOGY OF THE CHILD

1. Three Ways of Diagnosing 3

2. Some Guiding Images in the Area
   of Motor Disturbances:
   The Lonely Individual 15

3. Some Guiding Images in the Area
   of Sensory Disturbances 31

4. The Problem of Right and Left 45

5. The World of Language 59

6. The *Gestalt* of the Child..73

PART II

EPILEPSY AND HYSTERIA

1. An Introduction to Convulsive Disorders..........87

2. Different Types of Convulsive Disorders 103

3. Epilepsy and Hysteria..117

Notes..133

Foreword

Through the lectures by Karl König presented in this volume, readers encounter an inspired doctor and curative educator who devoted his whole life to the medicine and pedagogy that arose out of the impulse of Rudolf Steiner's anthroposophy.

For Karl König, curative diagnostics means the striving to come to a true understanding of an individual's special destiny and developmental conditions and to use that understanding as a basis for learning how best to help that person on his or her path through life.

The second through fifth lectures describe the basic preconditions for a human being's incarnation: achieving mobility, relating to attributes of the environment through the sense organs, orienting one's body and mind in space, learning to speak, and understanding the human form as an expression of an individual's readiness to incarnate as well as of his or her character.

For the most part, these lectures, given in 1965, have not lost any of their relevance although, for instance, König's recommendations for dealing with left-handed children no longer apply, having been based in part on a view of neurophysiological functions that has been superseded in recent decades by new research in this area (see also note 5 in chapter 4). Even today, however, König's lectures can help us recognize even the most severely handicapped person's intrinsic dignity and quality of life and can help us see meaning in and understand even the most difficult destinies.

This little book should help many curative educators,

as well as parents and teachers, to better understand and love the children entrusted to them.

Dornach, Switzerland   MICHAELA GLÖCKLER, M.D.

Medical Section of the
Free School for Spiritual Science
at the Goetheanum

Introduction

As issues and needs in the realm of education, and particularly curative education, continue to multiply and become increasingly complex, a fundamental contribution like these nine lectures becomes a welcome and necessary addition to the available literature. Although the content of this book was delivered as two series of lectures over twenty-five years ago, they are both fresh and poignant today and, no doubt, will be in future years as well for parents, therapists, educators, professionals and others concerned with basic issues of recognizing and understanding the various symptoms and irregularities with individuals who call for special soul care and insight.

Thus we are pleased to present this book in English, as it has been a greatly treasured resource for many years in the German edition. We are especially pleased to make this book available on the occasion of the 50th anniversary, in June, 1990, of the Camphill Movement, which Dr. Karl König founded near Aberdeen, Scotland. Perhaps this publication could be counted among the various celebrations of this anniversary year, not so much because of any specific reference to the community and the therapeutic work of Camphill, but because such a publication has emanated, as it were, from the activities and efforts with which Camphill has been concerned for fifty years. It is fitting that actually two publications by Karl König will be issued in conjunction with this anniversary; this one, focussing on fundamental diagnostic guidelines, and another on social threefoldness. Both orientations lie close to the basic and primary principles Dr. König brought into the community striving of Camphill.

There were a number of people who helped support this edition of *Being Human: Diagnosis in Curative Education*. Catherine Creeger translated the lectures from German with great perseverance and dedication. Her participation in this project has been enduring and invaluable. Also the encouragement from the trustees of Dr. König's archive, Nick Poole and Michael Luxford, helped expedite the publication, as did the active and full support of Michael Dobson, our publisher, who immediately recognized the importance of this work to the English-speaking anthroposophical community. Both Christof-Andreas Lindenberg and Ingo Maier have also been active in preparing this edition for publication.

Many have awaited these lectures for years, knowing that *Diagnosis in Curative Education* addresses specific and urgent problems. Slowly, and following the incredible gift of Rudolf Steiner's *Curative Course* given in 1924 on the occasion of his visit to the Lauenstein home, an increasing amount of material has become available to readers of English. Aside from *Children in Need of Special Care* (Thomas Weihs), the now out-of-print *Aspects of Curative Education* (ed. Carlo Pietzner), the so-called "Village Lectures" by Dr. König published as *In Need of Special Understanding*, booklets like *Questions of Destiny* (Carlo Pietzner), and the work of Dr. Walter Holtzapfel, there are several privately published monographs available to those looking for guidelines and help in the area of special needs. Indeed, in the last ten years, perhaps concomitant with an ever greater manifestation of special needs among our brothers and sisters, an increasing amount of literature has become available. *Diagnosis in Curative Education* is a major and significant contribution to the area of curative education and social therapy as well as to the vast and challenging area of abnormality and irregularity of being in general. It is an important work by one of the great personalities in this area of endeavor, a humanitarian and doctor who gained tremendous insights into being human through his devotion and love for individuals in need of special soul understanding.

August 1989   Cornelius M. Pietzner

PART I

The Anthropology of the Child

1. Three Ways of Diagnosing

What is curative education, anyway? There is no simple response to this question, and it can be answered differently on different levels. However, most of you will probably agree when I call curative education a "practical art." I think that's accurate enough, because we're dealing with creative activity whenever we practice curative education. Anyone who really wants to be effective in this field knows there are no set rules on how to do things in curative education. We must always be innovative and creative in relating to each child or adult, otherwise it doesn't work. And just because curative education is a practical art, whatever we do must always be new and creative, responding to the situation of the moment.

That's one side of the coin. On the other hand, if curative education were nothing more than a practical art, none of us would be good curative educators. We also need a background of practical knowledge to constantly replenish us in our creative activity. Perhaps describing this kind of knowledge will open one of the doors into true curative education for us.

This course is about diagnosis in curative education. Literally, diagnosis means "knowing something through and through," and it's in this sense of the word that I would like to consider what we mean by curative diagnostics. It should not mean simply being able to name and describe each child's condition—names are just so many empty words. The crucial element in curative-educational diagnostics seems to me to be the effort we make to understand whatever confronts us in each individual child, "through and through."

However, we do need to concern ourselves more precisely with the actual term itself. Curative education is a young art and a still younger science that had its conscious origins at a definite point in time. Its inception in the late 1700s coincided with the awakening of the ideals of liberty, equality, and fraternity that led not only to the French Revolution but also to German Idealism as represented by Fichte, Schelling, Hegel, and others. At that time, what we now know as curative, remedial, or special education was just beginning. People like Séguin, Guggenbühl, Pestalozzi, and others in France and Switzerland were the first to initiate this kind of healing education, which eventually grew to encompass the tremendous amount of knowledge and activity belonging to the field of curative education as we know it today. The scope of this development in all the civilized nations of the world is so monumental that we still don't know exactly what we're dealing with.

Nowadays we have many different names for this vast field. In Germany, it's been called Heilpädagogik, "curative education," for over a hundred years. Today, however, we can also use the modern term "child psychiatry." In the English-speaking countries, it's known as the field of mental deficiency. We know that none of these three terms actually encompasses the totality, and we also realize, if sometimes only vaguely or half-consciously, that we need to know about this all-embracing field for the sake of our practical and creative activity. But what is it really? Perhaps you'll know what I mean if I call it a "comprehensive child anthropology." But then of course you'll ask, "Why child anthropology? Wouldn't that describe the normal or average course of child development? Why should that be the all-inclusive element in true curative education?"

Simply because all the deviant conditions, illnesses, personality disturbances and physical deformities we meet are nothing more than details in the overall anthropology of the child we need as a background if we want to be real curative educators. Child psychiatry, for example, deals with psycho-physical deviations; the field of mental deficiency deals with intellectual retardation; special or remedial education addresses the question of practical and theoretical help for children with any form of developmental delay. All three are part of the greater unity I tried to describe in a nutshell by calling it "comprehensive child anthropology," an anthropology of the growing and developing child. This is the background we need if our study of the different stages and processes of child development is to equip us with the necessary guiding images and personal qualities to sustain our attempts at working artistically and formatively on the child who is the object of our attention.

In arriving at a curative-educational diagnosis, the point is not only to see the deviations, but to see them against the mighty backdrop of a comprehensive child anthropology. After all, what we perceive as pathological, abnormal, or deviant is nothing falling outside the scope of normal development. We must simply look for the point along the way where, in the course of a development that includes all the elements of normality, it began to become abnormal.

We can only gain true insight into the method of diagnosis in curative education by describing its negative, that is, by drawing conclusions about what it is on the basis of what it is not. That's why we'll also need to describe medical and psychological methods of diagnosis. Please don't interpret this negatively—I only want to describe how physicians and psychologists arrive at their diagnoses so we can understand the process. What is the difference between these methods of diagnosing? Where do we draw the line between medical, psychological, and curative-educational diagnoses? I know it's not easy, but we must try to learn to make these distinctions.

Let me read you a passage on medical diagnosis from an excellent child psychiatry text by Lutz, who is also concerned with these distinctions.[1] We can sense the urgency and dissatisfaction in his statement that "in medicine, it is often possible to describe an illness in one or two words, such as gastroenteritis, athlete's foot, weeping eczema, diabetes, etc. In child psychiatry, attempts at a similar nomenclature have failed." This points significantly to the fact that simply diagnosing an illness is not the whole point in curative education. Of course you can say that a certain child is suffering from aftereffects of encephalitis. That's a medical diagnosis, and although it's certainly necessary for curative education, it tells you only one thing about that child. As a curative educator, you have nothing to go by unless you can recall the symptoms usually related to post-encephalitic syndrome, thus adding something yourself to the diagnosis of encephalitis.

What does this really mean? It means that in medicine it's not primarily the patient who is being diagnosed, but the illness. The physician's chief concern is to find out what the person is suffering from, whether it's an infectious disease or a pathological condition such as asthma, nephritis, an ulcer, or any other of the thousands of possibilities. But as soon as I, as a doctor, have discovered that it's pneumonia, for instance, something else happens—I become a therapist and prescribe a medication. I know there are thousands and thousands of doctors today who realize that pneumonia is different in each different personality who comes down with it, and who treat not just the pneumonia but the individual who has it. But for the most part, medical diagnosis is still primarily concerned with the disease itself.

Psychological diagnosis is something totally different and starts with a completely different set of assumptions. Once again, I beg you to believe that I have the greatest respect for this kind of diagnosis as long as it isn't taken to be the one and only valid factor. Psychological diagnosis is not at all concerned with illnesses, the patient's reactions, or medications. Its only concern is to establish a coherent picture of someone's behavior, to gain insight into the condition of that person's psyche. It would be beside the point to ask whether a particular person has liver or kidney trouble, brain damage or sensory disturbances; a true psychological diagnostician more or less disregards all that while examining a person's behavior independent of whatever else may present itself.

Psychological testing puts a child or adult into a specific situation in which he or she is given certain problems to solve or is given an opportunity for self-expression. You know how it confronts a person with certain tasks, the performance of which provides the basis for coming to certain conclusions about his or her "intelligence," although I use this current term with some reservations. You know as well as I do that any number of so-called intelligence tests have been developed in America, Britain, Switzerland, Germany— all of them more or less refinements of Binet's original. These tests present questions or problems for people to solve so that how they express themselves in this situation can be examined. Their attention span, memory, powers of observation and concentration, motor skills, speed, and reactions can be tested in endless variety, depending on the individual choice of the psychologist. That's one kind of test.

Then there's another variety of tests called personality or projective tests, which are much more important than I.Q. tests, although still very questionable as to how they are applied and the insights they yield. What happens in a projective test? Let's take the oldest one, the Rorschach or inkblot test. It confronts the subject with something undefined, something not immediately identifiable. And since human beings are creative beings, after all, the subject begins to develop all kinds of imaginative combinations based on these black and white or sometimes even colored inkblots. The responses are all noted down, and from them, out of their great experience, the Rorschach specialists can deduce something, and often something very significant, about the personality structure of the child or adult in question.

For example, take the Szeno Test, which I believe is widely used in Germany. It provides an opportunity for creative self-expression, and the way a child combines or places objects and the stories he or she makes up about them begin to reveal certain aspects of his or her personality. This is important, of course, but basically it has nothing to do with a curative-educational diagnosis. Many people distrust these tests; Lutz, Asperger, and many other special-education experts don't set much store by them, calling them a help but nothing more. And if you ask me why, I can only find one answer: it's because the examiners, the psychologists, are actually not sufficiently aware of the extent to which they themselves influence the test situation.

Just a few years ago, a comprehensive investigation was carried out at a famous London clinic and published under the title *Night Call*.[2] What it describes is the situation of physicians, general practitioners, who have to make house calls at night. The interesting thing these studies show is not that people make up all kinds of excuses for calling a doctor at all hours of the night simply because it doesn't cost them anything in Britain any more, but that the physicians' state of mind has a significant influence on the people calling them. For lack of a better word, it's as if there were some kind of telepathic connection between patient and doctor. It's not just that the patient needs help and then calls the doctor; the patient calls the doctor when the doctor needs to be called out at night. It's hard to believe that a doctor can need to be called out at night, but I tell you, that's actually the way it is. The physicians become aware of the fact that they have to confront themselves in order to help the patients, who may hardly need help at all but are actually helping the doctors.

Let me give you an example. Once I left Camphill in Scotland and took the sleeper train from Aberdeen because I had urgent business in London. I had been in the grips of a deep depression for days and didn't know how I was going to make it through the night, alone with my depression in that box of a sleeping car. But even before the train left the station, the conductor came through calling, "Is there a doctor on the train?" He knew me, so as soon as he saw me he said, "Oh, you're here! Please come right away—there's a child up there who's got a finger slammed in the door." I can still hear that three-year-old screaming as if it were today. I had medication on me, so I bandaged the finger and calmed down the child and the parents, too, and do you know what happened after that? I drifted peacefully off to sleep with a smile on my face! Now it would be ridiculous to say that child got a finger jammed in the door just for my sake, but it's true. That's the kind of thing we need to become aware of.

Nowadays we know, for instance, that patients in psychotherapy with Jungians have Jungian dreams, while the patients of Freudians have Freudian dreams and the patients of Adlerians, Adlerian dreams. This is nothing to laugh about. It points out the deep and direct connection existing between people, and we must not believe that we as psychologists can objectively assess what's going on in another person. Because of this interplay between examiner and examinee, it's simply impossible. There's a lovely story by Heinrich von Kleist about a puppet theater that illustrates what I mean. It describes what happens between a bear and a fencer— the bear knows exactly what movement to make even before the fencer raises his arm. Human beings are social creatures. They don't exist in isolation, they exist only in relationship to others, and fools who believe they can't be influenced, or don't want to be influenced, are sadly mistaken indeed. People only exist by continually renewing themselves through their influence on others and others' influence on them.

This fundamental realization paves the way for something essential to true diagnostics in curative education, namely for the insight that I as a human being am incapable of disregarding myself to such an extent that I can judge someone else objectively. This is not meant to pull the rug out from under all our knowledge and insights, and you would be misunderstanding me if you would therefore assume that everything is subjective. It is, of course, but why shouldn't it be? Isn't it ridiculous to think we always have to have objective insights? Isn't that a complete and utter prejudice? Why shouldn't we have subjective ways of looking at things? We must reach the point where we realize, for instance, that although an electroencephalogram may tell us a lot about the electrical currents in a human brain, it is influenced just as strongly by the examiner as by the patient being examined.

Statistical inquiries into the social background of a child, an adult, or a whole stratum of society always need to be interpreted, and they're always changed in the interpretation, because even if the numbers, the findings, come from a computer, they've still been oriented and arranged in accordance with what the person who did it was thinking, feeling, and perceiving, both consciously and unconsciously. Even a double-blind test, so often required these days, depends entirely on the interpretation of those who think they can pull the wool over other people's eyes. The idea of objective diagnosis or of objective science altogether has just about been taken to the point of absurdity. By now, you find it only in textbooks. Real scientists who have even just a little philosophical and psychological insight into what they're doing are beginning to realize that human beings are indeed the measure of all things. When I, a subjective human being, stand in front of a patient or deal with a child or examine someone to be tested, when I observe plants or animals or stars, then I myself am the standard against which all these things are measured.

As soon as we begin to understand this, we know, to quote Nicholas Cusanus, that we know nothing, but that in knowing nothing we find the focal point of our existence, namely, that we are the measure of all things, because there is no other way. Only then do we begin to be curative diagnosticians, because then we know that the same all-encompassing anthropology of human existence that stands behind us also stands behind each child or adult to be diagnosed. As soon as I know myself as an individual in whom everything else is reflected, each child in my surroundings, each child I approach, begins to be mirrored in me, for example. This is not something I may "assess," but if I want to diagnose curatively, I must stay as alive and vital as the child and must realize out of this same vitality that I am mirrored in the child just as much as the child is mirrored in me. In fact, we are all both examiners and examinees, therapists and patients, in constant alternation. I am not "above" and the child "below"; we are there for and with each other. The only difference is that in my dealings with the child, I have to have some knowledge the child cannot yet have. Returning to Kleist's imagery, the child reacts instinctively like the bear, while I as the fencer must at least have some inkling of how to handle the sword. When we become aware that examiner and examinee share a common ground, that both are simultaneously active and passive, and when in addition this all-encompassing anthropology begins to come alive in us, step by step, then we begin to become curative diagnosticians.

We know that what physicians give us will be a neurological diagnosis, psychologists will offer us a personality test and tell us about the child's intelligence, teachers will tell us something about the child's achievements, and social workers will provide information on the child's family background. These assessments are all part of the picture and all need to be considered, but no single one of them is valid or sufficient by itself. It needs a whole group of people to bring these things together in an attempt at understanding, and each member of the group must know that this encounter with the child is at least as significant for him or her as it is for the child in question. They are not only assessing the child; the child is also assessing them at the same time. Once we have achieved this as a basic attitude, we will be at the beginning, but only the very beginning, of being able to come to a truly curative diagnosis.

Of course we have to acquire knowledge, but we should not do so by studying only deviations or pathological conditions, so that we speak of deaf, spastic, mongoloid, or encephalitic children as if their condition existed in isolation. Instead, for example, we should gain our knowledge from a general study of motor activity in children and then go on to attempt to diagnose motor disturbances. We need to understand the anthropology of children's sensory activity first before deducing anything about vision and hearing deficits and related conditions. We need to study the anthropology of the right/left polarity first, and then go on to try to understand its disturbances such as midline defects, twinning, lefthandedness, and so on. We should try to thoroughly research the threefold human organism from a general anthropological point of view, and only then attempt to grasp the conditions of hydrocephaly and microcephaly. We will look at all of these things in the lectures to come.

We must always keep in mind that the children and adults in our care are not there to be talked about and looked down upon as something separate from ourselves. They belong to us, because we also carry this very hydrocephaly or microcephaly, midline defect, or whatever the deviation may be, in ourselves. Such anomalies are simply more obvious, more clearly revealed, in these children than they usually are in us. We must realize that we are all potential epileptics or latent psychopaths; we all conceal autistic or schizophrenic traits that have not yet become apparent. In knowing this, we take the first steps toward awakening in ourselves this all-encompassing anthropology of child development so that we can recognize ourselves when we behold a handicapped adult or child with special needs. For, just like any other human being, I too am individual and subjective and the measure of all things.

2. Some Guiding Images in the Area of Motor Disturbances

The Lonely Individual

Yesterday we tried to work out what's unique about curative educational diagnosis, comparing it both to the diagnostic efforts of psychology and to the way a medical diagnosis is usually attempted. We were primarily concerned with the insight that in curative diagnostics in particular, the diagnostician as a subjective being is an active and legitimate part of the diagnosis. Although we always imagine that a diagnostician can objectively determine the facts of a case, this is actually not possible. Every diagnosis is influenced by the diagnostician and, to take it one step further, the one who diagnoses is part of what needs diagnosing. Believing that such a thing as objective diagnosis is possible, through some kind of statistical evaluation or whatever, in no way frees us from this situation. We must include ourselves as belonging to the diagnostic process. Only when we act out of this recognition can we approach what may be called a curative-educational diagnosis.

Yesterday we used the expression that the human being is the measure of all things. There's no getting away from that. It's interesting to note that child psychiatrists like Tramer and Lutz say that any diagnosis in curative education must actually be a multifactorial one. Let me read you a passage from the chapter on diagnostics in Lutz's textbook. He says:

In accordance with the present state of research and prevailing professional opinion, child psychiatry is tending toward multidimensional (Tramer), multifactorial diagnosis and thus dispenses with one-word labels in the majority of cases. The attempt is made to replace the diagnosis with a description such as one of the following: "Cultural-familial retardation in a socially deprived adolescent girl born out of wedlock" or "Child in defiant phase showing regressive bed-wetting following sister's birth; neuropathic tendencies" or "Schoolboy with parents eager for retirement; tearful/hypochondriacal underachiever suffering from aftereffects of concussion (headaches, sensitivity to weather changes)."[1]

This is important because it is attempting something that is not yet possible, namely, to come up with a really comprehensive curative educational diagnosis. They're trying to present the whole social, medical, psychological, and curative-educational background of a child or adolescent, and rightly so. Why is that necessary? Because unless we feel our way from all possible points of the compass, we can't possibly begin to comprehend a child in his or her development (or lack of development) and total life-situation.

I tried to bring to your attention yesterday the need to acquire a broad background for our curative-educational diagnosis, a background we characterized as a comprehensive anthropology of the child. We must carry this panorama of comprehensive child anthropology with us whenever we want to attempt to understand any child with or without developmental delays. Then we diagnosticians must summon up the courage to insert ourselves into the picture and show what we actually want to select from the broad context of comprehensive child anthropology. In observing, listening to, and empathizing with a child, we must learn which melodies—and the choices are infinite—we are willing to play on this keyboard. I use the word "willing" because the melody will necessarily be different for each one who tries to assess such a child. The doctor's melody will be different from the teacher's, the psychotherapist's from the curative educator's, and the musician's from the craft instructor's, but effective curative education becomes possible only when all these melodies are similar and in harmony with each other. It would be totally ineffective if a doctor would lay claim to the only correct diagnosis and a teacher would counter with a different diagnosis, insisting that it's the only appropriate one. The way a doctor listens to a child is different from a teacher's perception and from the way a curative educator feels the child out, and only all of them together can make up a kind of diagnostic symphony in which the individuality of the child can begin to appear. When we do this, we are not merely making the child an object of our observation, but already begin to work with him or her in a therapeutically helpful and formative way, simply through the diagnostic process itself.

We must learn that in pronouncing a psychological, medical, or curative-educational diagnostic judgment, we are not pronouncing an absolute, but that it can always only be a subjective interpretation in which the one who's doing the assessing is just as deeply involved as the one assessed. Meaningful action and meaningful intervention will result only once we get used to taking this attitude toward life, because only then can destiny take effect between child and therapist, patient and doctor, or between the curative educator and the child in care. I as a single individual am necessarily subjective; while it's possible to *think* objectivity, it's not actually possible to achieve it. This is an insight that will have to evolve more and more in the hearts and minds of human beings in the course of this century. And if I enter into a therapeutic, pedagogical, or curative-educational process in full awareness of the fact that I as a human being am "the measure of all things," then something good will come of it.

It's all a question of finding guiding images, of feeling our way toward the all-encompassing manifoldness of child anthropology; the more we learn about it, the more octaves of the keyboard we'll be able to play on. If we speak only of child psychology or of a child's neuromuscular system, we'll have only a very small section of the keyboard at our disposal. But if, for example, we take all of the child's growth and development into consideration, if we know that a developing child never stands still but is constantly on the verge of something new, if we go back even to before birth to trace development in the womb, if we make a thorough study of embryology, then images become available for us to select at the appropriate moment, and melodic structures evolve that begin to resound when we look at a particular person.

Let me give you some examples. Down's syndrome can be understood only if you go way back into the time before birth and notice that every mongoloid child bears certain embryonic features. And you won't be able to understand a harelip if you don't know from studying embryology that different parts of the human face grow toward each other, and that when they don't come together completely, a cleft remains in the lip or even in the palate and jaw. There's a condition called hypertelorism, almost unknown here in Germany, in which a person's whole face stays broad in the middle, so that the two sides of the nose scarcely come together and the eyes look out on both sides almost like those of a horse. If you've studied embryology, then you know that the face of an embryo looks just like this in a certain specific week in its development when the human countenance has not yet grown together into a unified whole. Then images from developmental stages of the distant past can enter our daily existence, because the whole structure of these people's souls and emotions, as well as of their bodies, is such that they offer reminders of earlier stages of existence to present-day humanity.

And in looking at developmental stages after birth, you'll need to know, for instance, how Rudolf Steiner describes a child's first three years: how a child begins to acquire uprightness, developing motor activity in the process; how the motor activity of speech gradually emerges out of general motor development so that the mother tongue can be imitated; how the first forms of conceptualization and reflection develop out of and through language—in short, how the movements of speech and, ultimately, of thinking arise out of the general acquisition of movement. If this isn't accessible to curative educators at all times, then what are they going to base their diagnosis on?

Think about how every child over the age of three must gradually develop an individual and particular orientation in the world with regard to right and left; how dominance arises in hand, leg, eye, and ear out of this right/left orientation, so that orientation in space and in the world in general can come about. If we don't constantly apply this knowledge, or if we forget its importance, then we aren't able to describe the anthropology of human development completely.

What if you forget or fail to take into account what it means that a developing human being begins to smile as soon as he or she turns toward the world, or if you don't attempt to grasp at least to some extent the expressive possibilities and realities revealing themselves in a little thing like a smile— smiles of greeting, of embarrassment, of fear, of attraction, of aversion, of irony? How, then, will you be able to comprehend the smile of a spastic child? What if you're not interested in the anthropology of laughing and crying, of screaming, shouting, and scolding? That's all part of comprehensive curative-educational diagnostics.

Observing a child's environment—the father's influence, the mother's ability or inability to offer guidance, the siblings and grandparents, the native language, the people and nation, the climatic conditions and type of landscape or "non-landscape" where the child grew up—all this is simply the necessary basis for a comprehensive curative-educational diagnostics. The tapestry of each individual's life is incomprehensibly manifold and mighty. Let me repeat that coming to a curative-educational diagnosis means mastering the keyboard and striking very particular tones in the right way and in the right moment.

Now let's turn to our theme for today and try to get an overview of motor disturbances. We don't want to get involved in medical diagnostics—that is, we don't want to debate what part of the brain has been damaged. That's beside the point as far as we're concerned at the moment. We only want to look at the phenomena, and we'll stick to Goethe's saying that there's no need to look behind the phenomena since they themselves are the teachers. So let's try to look at motor activity as a whole.

The anthropology of a child's movement is a very broad area, and we can't do better than to advise a budding curative educator not to neglect to observe how a child moves. But not only to observe it superficially and then say, "Well, he's a bit clumsy," or "She fidgets a lot," but to try to arrive at an image of this motor activity,

If you are interested in other publications of the Anthroposophic Press (including over 150 titles by Rudolf Steiner) please return this postcard.

Name _____

Address _____

City _____ State _____ Zip _____

Country _____

PLACE STAMP HERE

ANTHROPOSOPHIC PRESS
RR 4, BOX 94 A1
HUDSON, NEW YORK 12534-9420

because motor activity as the sum total of a person's movements is an expression of his or her personality and individuality. From our first breath to our last, from morning till night, our motor system is constantly engaged. We're constantly expressing ourselves by means of it. We simply can't help expressing ourselves through our movements while we walk and talk, move and write, cross the street, get up, eat, or do any of the many other things that are there to be done from morning till night, because as human beings we are doers. But the wonderful thing about movement is that it's not simply performing deeds; in every action the character of the doer is revealed immediately. There's a kind of graphology or physiognomy of movement—movement characters we must learn to read.

Each movement of a finger or of the head, every gesture accompanying what we say, lifting a glass of water, taking a step—each of these is a comprehensive portrayal of the individuality concerned. An actor is only really good when he not only tries to disguise himself, as we do for Halloween, but also learns to master his movements anew in the disguise. One of the most crucial things for an actor is to be able to master his movements so that he can be a devil or an old man or a young lover or whatever, right down into the movements. It's easy to give a wonderful speech and let your arms hang by your sides, but it isn't good enough. No one will believe you. Either you're telling the truth, in which case you tell it with the sum total of movements at your disposal, or you're faking it, and people will notice.

We are already approaching a person's inner being when we take in and diagnose the way he or she moves. Are her movements rounded or angular, tense or loose? Is he clumsy, invariably hitting his finger instead of the nail with his hammer, or can he arrange things perfectly

21

without even looking? All these things reveal the essential being within the motor system. Of course, there are many other things that reveal someone's inner being, but let's concentrate on motor activity for a while.

If we want to develop guiding images in the area of movement, it won't work if we impose classifications from outside the realm of movement. We have to try to gain an understanding of motor activity from the process of movement itself. We can only come to a fundamental understanding of motor activity when we begin to look at it as a musical process. I don't want to go into great detail, but I will point out a few aspects of this relationship between music and movement.

One aspect is the following: When children begin to acquire uprightness from the head down in the course of their first year of life, first lifting their head, then moving it freely, learning to support themselves on their arms, lifting their back and sitting unsupported, getting their feet and legs onto the ground more and more until they become aware of standing upright—in this whole process, children are doing nothing more than developing their instruments for the music of movement. You can imagine this instrument however you like, as a violin or cello or something else. People in earlier times were well aware of this. There are archaic representations of human beings that reveal immediately that the artists recognized head and torso as an instrument. This upright instrument, which more or less assumes its final form during the first year of life, and in and through which the child learns to maintain equilibrium against the forces of gravity, is the first thing we need to distinguish. It has relatively little to do with movement as yet, but a lot to do with posture.

At the same time, of course, though it's not so much in the foreground, the child begins to move. Muscle tone develops. Whether it's too strong or too weak, too slack or too tight, depends on the sort of development this individuality undergoes or on the presence of some disturbance. We're not interested right now in what that disturbance may be. But what does the development of muscle tone mean? It means that the tension on the infinite number of strings (muscles and tendons) belonging to this instrument is correct or incorrect, tight or slack. It means that whether a movement is stiff or flowing, angular or sloppy, depends on the tension of the strings, which is something different from the instrument itself. We'll still see how the instrument and the tension of its strings can work together. But then motor activity can begin to play on this instrument; melodies or movement patterns begin to develop. In the course of childhood and adolescence we gradually master them so that we eventually have them at our disposal and can put them to use.

This process continues right through childhood and youth and on into middle age. It has to, because we can only remain creative human beings as long as we're always trying to master new movement patterns, creating them within us. For instance, if we come to a particularly complicated point in our lives where we don't know how to go on, we might decide that as of tomorrow we're going to try to change our handwriting or learn a craft or do painting. This is nothing more than an attempt to awaken new movement patterns in ourselves.

The instrument, the tension on the strings, and playing the melodies of movement all contribute to motor activity. Modern physiology, not the textbook variety but real modern physiology, knows perfectly well by now that motor activity is not built up out of isolated movements such as reflexes but consists of nothing other than "melodies"— movement patterns, that is. If I want to pick up a glass of water, I can't piece together the act of picking it up out of individual movements. From head to toe, my whole motor being forms a counterbalance to my moving arm, and the whole thing makes up one movement pattern. If these movement patterns don't develop, if melodies like this can't be played on the instrument, then we speak of deterioration or lack of development of the motor system.

After all this, let's turn to the different kinds of cerebral palsy.[2] Over the centuries there have been two cerebral-palsied children born for every thousand births, approximately. People have tried to divide up and categorize the different forms of cerebral palsy, but that's terribly difficult to do because of course every cerebral-palsied child is an individuality too, and, to quote Phelps, "You scarcely find one resembling another," even if you've seen thousands. In general, however, we speak of paraplegia, quadriplegia, and another form called hemiplegia. Most of you will be more or less familiar with expressions like these. Hemiplegia is confined to one side of the body, either the right or the left; paraplegia usually affects the two lower extremities; quadriplegia is a paralysis affecting all four limbs—that is, almost the whole voluntary muscular system is involved.

It's easy to say that one child has paraplegia and another has hemiplegia or quadriplegia. But if you really want to look at this and understand it, then you ought to know that hemiplegia is a disturbance in the interplay between right and left, paraplegia a disturbance in the interplay between up and down, and quadriplegia, which affects everything, a disturbance in the relationship of front and back. As soon as we've said that, we begin to notice that hemiplegia, paraplegia, and quadriplegia have less to do with cerebral localization—that is, with the location of the brain damage—than with the person's integration into three-dimensional space. The paraplegic isn't properly integrated into the up/down relationship, the hemiplegic into right/left, or the quadriplegic into forward/back. As soon as you accept this, you'll already have a basis for proceeding from diagnosis to curative-educational practice, namely by trying to integrate the paraplegic into up and down, the hemiplegic into right and left, and the quadriplegic into forward and back.

So here we have these three forms of paralysis. We don't know very much about them yet, but we'll have an immediate intuitive grasp of them as soon as I've told you something that might sound ridiculous, but just because it's so dumb, it contains the whole (subjective) truth—my own stupid truth. You know what I mean.

All children are born "cerebral-palsied" as a matter of course, since at first none of us can stand or sit or do anything else. Each one of us was cerebral-palsied at some point, but we managed to overcome this paralysis step by step through acquiring uprightness, speech, and so on. As long as that's not clear to us, we won't grasp what's really involved when we meet children like that. What we're meeting is something actually belonging to infancy, but retained in later stages of life. That means we need to have the anthropology of child development in mind as a backdrop. We'll leave the necessary search for neurological impairment to medical diagnosis. But as curative educators trying to understand a paralyzed child, what we need to see is that he or she is still at a stage we were all in for a shorter or longer period after birth. If we were to go back still further, into the time before birth, to the second or third month of embryonic development, we'd find we had no limbs at all. Even at birth, the head/limb relationship is still such that we wouldn't manage to walk even if we did know how in theory. The relationship of a newborn's huge head to its tiny limbs and the great preponderance of the whole sensory system would make standing and walking impossible. During the first year of life, the limbs grow much faster than the head, and development "helps make a child ripe for the earth," to use an expression of Rudolf Steiner's, who made us aware of this image. Having and using limbs means being ready for the earth. Now, you see, this doesn't happen to cerebral-palsied children, who scarcely undergo any development at all because their limbs don't make it out of the stage characteristic of infancy. What does that signify?

Just a little while ago we talked about the "instrument" of a child's body and its relationship to posture. The disturbance called ataxia (failure of the balance-regulating system) means that the instrument cannot be perfected. Acquiring balance, or, more precisely, successfully integrating gravity into our physical nature, does not take place. Ataxics have to struggle constantly to maintain upright posture (a matter of course to the rest of us) by means of the senses of self-movement and touch. That means that ataxic children may learn to walk at age nine or ten months by hanging onto the sides of their playpen, but they never reach the stage of twelve to fourteen months, where they would have fully mastered carrying themselves over the face of the earth in a state of equilibrium.

The spastic is a person whose instrument may be perfectly well-formed, but because its strings aren't properly strung, no melodies, no movement patterns come about. It all still works to some extent if only the arms are involved, but if both the arms and the legs, or even just the legs are affected, then the instrument is so contracted by the tension on its strings that, although these people can still take hold of their own body, they can't use it as a means of penetrating space, if you see what I mean.

Paraplegics don't take part in gravity and buoyancy, in the interplay between up and down; quadriplegics don't take part in the interplay between forward and back; hemiplegics don't take part in the interplay between right and left. We'll still hear later how these directions in space are not simply equivalent and inter-changeable—up and down are qualitatively different from front and back or right and left. It's thoughts like this that make diagnostics come alive.

How is it with athetotics, who suffer from a movement disorder characterized by gestures which constantly overshoot the mark? Athetotics can certainly stand upright and move around, but impulses not belonging to them shoot through their movements again and again. It might help us to understand this if we put it as follows: Athetotics are human beings who move or are moved not only by the "I," the ego, but also by the "It." They have no means of controlling their movements or seeing them through to the end. For instance, when they want to pick something up, all kinds of movement impulses shoot through them which, although they do belong to them, are not ego-filled. When these people want to speak, their speech organs overcome them before they get started, instead of the other way around. This is no different from the many varied movements an infant makes in beginning to wiggle and kick around. That's natural athetosis, just as the completely harmonious paralysis of a still younger baby is a natural spasticity that's gradually overcome by the ego as the instrument is taking shape, the strings are stretched, and the first melodies of movement patterns are played.

We could go on talking about this indefinitely, but let me just add one more thing to bring our considerations to a close. You see, if you apply a certain attentiveness and devotion when you look at children who have become spastic or athetotic, and see how they aren't integrated into space, how they sit in their chairs smiling and noticing things and trying to make contact with other people, then you'll notice that these are human beings in isolation. There's no contact disturbance in children like this (as we'll learn to distinguish tomorrow). Their contact with the many people around them is good, and yet they're still lonely beings, through and through. That's why the subtitle of today's lecture is "The Lonely Individual." They aren't lonely because of lack of contact with other human beings. They're lonely because they are only minimally involved in what the earth offers us directly and immediately by way of gravity and light, air, warmth, cold, life and sound, becoming and dying, just because their loss of limb activity keeps them from being integrated into the threefold structure of space. You'll be interested to know that people have learned that the way paralyzed children form concepts can't possibly be compared to the way normal children do. If paralyzed children have to draw a house, they draw a window somewhere and put the doors any old place; when they draw a person, the arms come out of the head or something like that. We see examples of this every day. It has nothing to do with their physical difficulty in getting forms down on paper. Their concepts of structure and form are disturbed; the formation of their own bodies and hence of their body image—the immediate experience of one's own body—is totally distorted, so it's as if children like that were actually surrounded by the most astonishing fairy-tale world.

There's a deeply moving, even shocking picture called "The Lonely One" by the well-known painter Chagall. An old Jew is sitting with the Torah scroll in his hand, and in the background (as is so often the case with Chagall) a cow is floating away and a cloud appears from somewhere or other. What lives in and around these children is something similar. The world is fragmented—cows float around in the sky, the cello's on the roof, the angel's head is down by its feet, and a man puts his hand down on the table and walks away without it. That's why so many of Chagall's figures have six or seven or eight fingers—it doesn't concern him at all, just as such details don't concern the lonely paralyzed child who is excluded from the ordering of space. That's why animals just float around, with a mother here and just the father's head there, and the people are so much bigger than the little houses. You see, Chagall painted athetotic, hemiplegic, paraplegic pictures. Once we begin to understand that, we begin to gain insight into the loneliness of these children. And out of this insight we can learn to engender up and down, right and left, forward and back, artistically and creatively in paralyzed children so as to bring them (at least to some extent) into the "It-reality" they can't incorporate by themselves, thus remaining lonely individuals for years on end. If we begin to look at motor disturbances in this way, then diagnosis can turn into therapy, a therapy I, as a human being and as the measure of all things, carry within me.

3. Some Guiding Images in the Area of Sensory Disturbances

When we tried to come to an understanding of motor disturbances yesterday, I believe it became painfully clear to all of us just how little can be said on a subject like that in such a short time. In one hour, you can't do much more than point out the infinite variety in what a curative-educational practitioner needs to know about motor disturbances alone.

You may have noticed that I made an effort to simply present phenomena without touching on medical diagnostics or talking about brain damage. And it may have been the first time you heard about the importance of the three dimensions of space in this connection—for instance, that a person with paraplegia (spastic paralysis in both legs) is suffering from a disturbance in the relationship between up and down, while in a hemiplegic (someone with one side paralyzed) the relationship between right and left is disturbed, and in a quadriplegic (someone who's paralyzed in all four limbs) something has gone wrong in the relationship between front and back. These dimensions of space are only interchangeable if you look at them geometrically, but as a curative educator, you must learn to know what it means if a quadriplegic child is always oriented exclusively toward the front and has no experience of "backward," of behind, or if a paraplegic child is more or less only at home in what's up above and can't incorporate what's down below—gravity, the earth, depth in every sense of the word—because his or her limbs aren't made for it. As so-called normal people, we don't experience these things consciously at all. They're so much a matter of course to us that we scarcely pay attention to them. But as soon as a deviation appears, what we otherwise take for granted appears as a tremendous revelation, and unless we learn to see it, we won't be able to offer sufficient help.

I'm always eager to point to child anthropology because it includes, for instance, the recognition that being spastic or hemiplegic or athetotic means more than just not being able to move. It means a total reordering of the human existence in question. It's easy to overlook the fact that spastics are different through and through, that they are not simply "just like me" except for the fact that I can still move my limbs. For example, modern textbooks will still tell you that children with cerebral palsy are paralyzed, and that some have sensory disturbances as well—that is, some are hard of hearing, some visually impaired, and so on. It's all well and good to realize that, but it still doesn't necessarily bring us to the point where we can see the total picture. Sensory and motor disturbances are part of that picture, but a paralyzed child's overall condition and his or her level of emotional experience and development also contribute to it, just as a mongoloid child is a unity and doesn't simply consist of a physical disturbance and possibly a couple of deviant psychological traits. What's crucial here is being able to come to a true curative-educational diagnosis, that is, to an understanding "through and through."[1] As soon as we start looking at motor disturbances, there's something else we must also look at in order to really understand the children in question. What enables us to take our place in the dimensions of up and down, forward and back, right and left isn't just the motor system. Sense perception is also ultimately involved. There's a certain kind of sensory perception, the perception of our own physical existence, which we all carry within us and take for granted to such an extent that we don't even notice it. It's actually still overlooked by modern physiology and anthropology.

Paralyzed children, whether they're athetotic, ataxic, spastic, or have rigid paralysis, all suffer from serious sensory disturbances in the area of the so-called bodily senses in addition to their motor disturbances. The all-encompassing bodily senses are what constantly lifts our physical nature up into consciousness, however dully. Rudolf Steiner was the only one to clearly and unambiguously describe and differentiate the four bodily senses.[2] He spoke of the sense of touch, life, self-movement, and equilibrium. These senses are more or less known to modern physiology already, but their importance is not sufficiently appreciated.

Let me describe them briefly. Through the sense of touch, we perceive the surface of our own physical existence. When we touch something, we're not experiencing our outer environment but simply a pressure, something external impinging on something internal. We experience ourselves as a body with boundaries.[3] I can't go into more detail than that. The sense of life lets us experience well-being. That's difficult to define, but where does it come from when you get up in the morning and notice how you feel? You experience your physical nature as being refreshed or not, tired, dull, miserable, or bursting with life, as the case may be. This is what we experience quite generally through the sense of life, which is very much dependent on blood circulation, for instance, and on the pressure of circulating fluids and many other things. The sense of self-movement gives us a constant dull sensation of the position of different parts of our body in relation to each other. You don't need to look to know whether a finger's bent or stretched out, or whether your arm is bent forward or backward—you live with the constant sensation of it. The sense of equilibrium, which isn't recognized as a sense at all by some people, tells us, not the relationship of different parts of the body to each other, but the relationship of our total physical being to the vertical direction in space. Why do I say that? This way of grasping one's own physical nature is a very basic experience and is more or less lacking in children with motor disturbances. You may have experienced either personally or vicariously for instance, what it means to lose your balance and then to fall, falling apart psychologically, too, in the process. Loss of the sense of equilibrium can even lead to suicide because it's intolerable to lose your bearings in the world or to see the world in motion around you, as happens in a certain form of loss of equilibrium. Some of you may have experienced what it's like to be seasick, really seasick to the point where you're absolutely ready to die because you can't stand it any more. That's what the loss of just one of the four bodily senses does to you.

If you see a post-encephalitic child with motor disturbances who always has to run around in a frenzy, touching everything, grabbing things without looking and tossing them away again, that's not a real motor disturbance. It means that the child's experience of the sense of self-movement is either too strong or not strong enough. Consider how paralysis in an older person may suddenly make one arm stiff and immovable. In that case, moving the arm is impossible not only because a motor disturbance is present, but also because awareness of that hand or arm has totally disappeared. I can only move it by taking hold of it with my healthy hand, just as I'd move any other object. It's like that with many spastic children—they'd be able to move if you could awaken their sense of self-movement so they could experience their hand again.

We hear so much nowadays about congenital metabolic disturbances that can lead to severe retardation in intellectual development. What's present in cases like these? For example, in phenylketonuria, in addition to specific disturbances in protein metabolism, the sense of life is also disturbed, and the child's experience of his or her own body no longer makes it possible to take possession of it.[4] Small children entering into their bodily organization step by step take possession of their bodies not only by learning to move their fingers, hands, eyes, head, neck, chest, and lower limbs, but primarily by acquiring a dull but fundamental underlying experience of their overall bodily organization. What I told you briefly yesterday about distortion and disturbance of "body image" in spastics and athetotics is actually due to the fact that the four lower senses of touch, life, self-movement, and equilibrium aren't functioning. Eventually physiologists will realize that body image is nothing more than these four senses put together. That's how it comes about. We could spend a lot of time talking about body image, but it needs to be taken a lot further than we can go at the moment.

What I tried to summarize about yesterday's topic can be condensed into a single word, and I beg you to use this expression more and more. It is "incarnation"—meaning that an individuality as it develops and unfolds takes possession of its bodily organization step by step. Please make a note of that. These steps in the incarnation process can be observed in every child. If you ask at what age a child lifted his or her head, sat up, stood up, walked independently and unsupported, and so on, you're tracing the steps of incarnation, of taking possession of the physical organization. But taking possession of our body isn't the only thing we do as we grow up. That's only half of it. Something else happens simultaneously, integrated into the process of incarnation. I'd like to give this other process a name, too—not as nice a name as "incarnation," perhaps, but it'll be something you can understand immediately. Let's call it "discrimination"—that is, a child learns to discriminate and distinguish between the objects and beings of the world. I take possession of my body: *incarnation*. I begin to grasp the world in such a way that I distinguish between the things and beings I encounter: *discrimination*.

You see, very small children or infants aren't really as asleep and unconscious as we always think they are. We've become painfully aware that infants are deeply dependent on what goes on in their environment, just because they're much more deeply integrated into the world than older children or adults. I repeat, babies and small children are much more deeply integrated into the world. It's just that their integration is a more general one. Max Scheler tried to point this out again and again in the early 1900s. He suspected that learning (not just learning in school, but learning in the broadest sense of the word) is merely the process of making more and more distinctions within the field of general perception. If you make that the basis of any curative-educational assessment of a child, if you learn that discriminating in the world and incarnating into the body are intimately related, then that is the curative diagnostic equivalent of beginning to grasp the Pythagorean Theorem in mathematics.

A small child learns how to focus, grasp, and walk, which are motor stages of incarnation. Meanwhile, however, the process of discrimination is also taking place. If I look out into the world and focus on an object, or if I pick it up and have it in my grasp, it becomes a single selected experience for me. And when I walk, I not only take steps, I also walk toward some object. We must try to understand how these developments go hand in hand.

A developing child's individuality actually takes two distinct steps. It takes the step into incarnation by beginning to take hold of the body, thus developing the four lower senses in connection with motor activity. Therefore, every motor disturbance is also a disturbance in the process of incarnation. The other step it takes is out into the world by means of the process of discrimination, by learning how to make distinctions. Of course, each of these steps takes its own direction. Incarnation into the body proceeds centrifugally, I would say, while discrimination takes the opposite direction. Everything is general at first; the child is embedded in the world as a whole. Then the curtain of general mythical experience is pierced bit by bit (if I may put it like that) and individual things and objects become visible through the holes. The child begins to distinguish between mother and father and siblings, to notice the window and what's fluttering around in the air—it takes a long time to learn to distinguish whether it's a fly or a butterfly or something else. That flowers can be different and that there's a difference between daisies and all other flowers is a distinction that's often not made until quite an advanced age. This development takes place gradually in children. To sum it up, we perceive the world step by step, through learning to make distinctions; we perceive our body through learning to experience it more and more as a totality, as "body image."

You see, an embryo develops out of a plethora of separate and very different contributing parts. For instance, the heart develops outside the embryo's body, the brain develops at first without any relationship to the other organs, the eyes grow from the inside out toward the surface and the ears from the outside in. In the course of embryonic development, this is all gradually consolidated and coordinated and becomes a body, which is then gradually unified by the four lower senses after birth, and becomes the basis for human existence. In contrast to this, the world gets taken apart, as it were, when a child begins to name individual parts of it during the second year of life. It's only when the first steps in conceptualization and thinking have been made that a child begins to connect these discriminated parts again. That's what's really involved in each child's development.

These two things, incarnation and discrimination, must be observed in every case. I've already spoken about the stages of motor development. But how do you recognize a child's waking up to his or her environment? You must ask mothers at what age, and how, their children smiled for the first time. When did they first stretch out their arms to be picked up? When did they first follow things with their eyes? When did they begin to respond to sounds? If you follow the course of discrimination further, you'll arrive at a very specific point where imitation begins. Imitation is just as neglected by child anthropology as the four lower senses are, although (as Rudolf Steiner pointed out conclusively) there's practically nothing as significant for a child's development as the power of imitation and the fact that the world is imitated by the child.

Yesterday, to conclude our discussion on motor disturbances, we spoke about the "lonely individual," and I tried to show you that it's not the person who has no contact with others who is lonely. Spastic children are lonely in spite of making contact because they're excluded from a whole realm I described yesterday, cut off from the whole realm of air, light, and earthly gravity, and placed in isolation. If you hear about a child who never smiled, for instance, never turned toward his or her surroundings and therefore never developed the possibility of independent creative imitation and play, then you'll know immediately that child is contact-disturbed.

Underline this sentence in red: Imitation is a preliminary stage of contact. The interplay between incarnation and discrimination brings about imitation, and real contact with other human beings develops by way of imitation and play. Contact is a developmental stage preceded by imitation and play. Wherever you find contact-disturbed children, whether they're autistic or psychotic or whatever, you'll notice that they possess neither the power of imitation nor the possibility of freely creative play. It's usually not because of a failure in the process of incarnation but rather because they haven't succeeded in discriminating and experiencing the world.

Two examples: First, blind or visually impaired children. Once again, blind children are not adequately described by simply saying they can't see. Blind children are different from sighted people right down into the roots of their existence, right down into their metabolism, as we've learned in the past twenty years. If you try to feel your way toward understanding the being of a blind child on the basis of what we've tried to explain here, what do you find? Obviously, because of pathological changes in the eyes, which may admit only a glimmer of light, any eye-related discrimination is missing. The child remains in an infantile discriminatory stage, experiencing the world mythically and generally, while incarnation proceeds a bit further. But because the eye doesn't become effective in separating and distinguishing objects in the world, and because the world doesn't come toward a blind person and take hold of him or her in a way that cultivates discrimination, you'll find, for instance, that the movements of blind children remain stereotyped and that a certain amount of anxiety and fear is always present in them. You'll only understand why blind children have this strange way of making faces all the time if you really take a look at what I've tried to present. They can't keep their faces still—their lips move, their eyes blink, their cheeks are contorted—and unless they're pulled to attention and made to concentrate on something specific, their faces are constantly in motion. A blind person's face is taken over by the motor activity of the whole body instead of being open to the world. It's often complicated to establish contact with blind children because they're way out in the world out there and can't achieve eye-to-eye contact at all. I mean it just the way I say it. The physical body of a blind child is a constant hindrance to contact.

A second example: Children who are deaf or hearing-impaired. Once again, much more is involved than the fact that they simply can't hear; their whole personal make-up is different. How they live in the world and in their own physical organization is diametrically opposed to how it is with blind people. You see, deaf people's eyes are wide awake; because their ears hear little or nothing, both discrimination and motor activity (taking hold of the body) are particularly strongly developed. You can really say that deaf people jump right into the world with their limbs and senses. They actually reach too deeply into the world and into their own bodies. In contrast, blind people only make timid efforts to penetrate their own bodies and what's around them in the world. If, in your empathy and desire to help, you can experience these people as not simply lacking vision or hearing, if you can experience blindness as timid, tentative, and listening, and deafness as aggressive in seeing and moving, then you'll know immediately that you must bring deaf people to stillness and help them learn to listen, and that you must take blind people and make them focus, gently, tenderly, but actively, so that they begin to take hold of their own bodies as well as the world. I know they won't learn to see, but they will be able to focus, which is different from seeing. And deaf children may also not learn to hear, but they will learn to listen. If this attitude becomes prevalent in schools for the deaf and blind, then they'll really be able to do some good.[5]

In this day and age, more and more children are growing up autistic, psychotic, or otherwise contact-disturbed. We won't investigate why just now, but we should ask ourselves what we're actually dealing with. What can we say about this now that we've looked at the blind and deaf as examples of people with sensory disturbances? What's really involved when a child doesn't smile or imitate or play anymore, but looks right through people and fails to develop any interpersonal relationships?

Most autistic children are so tightly squeezed into the world that they develop fixations on all space-time relationships. That is, the same thing has to happen at the same time every day, or they explode in desperation. An autistic child may always have to sit at the same place at the same table, and drink the same juice (or milk) from a cup which always has to be the same one—maybe red and green speckled. Any attempt to change a fixation like this brings on a screaming fit. What does that mean?

If you think that a person like that has no relationships and that his or her contacts with the world are disturbed, you've got it all backwards. Of course contact is disturbed, but not because the child has no connection to anything or anybody, but because the connection is much too strong. Children like this don't live in their bodies—

they live in the table, in the chair, in the daily routine, in the cup, in the milk, and in everything else that surrounds them. They're not fixed in their bodies, they're fixed in the objects and processes of their environment. It's all a question of relaxing this fixation, of helping children who say "I" to other people and "you" to themselves to get out of their fixations.

In the case of children like this, contact can't be established because there's one thing lacking—something we call "distance." They have no distance, just as an infant or very small child is still distance-less. Contact only comes about once a small child can fall down and get hurt and begin to weep or experience rejection and the first hard knocks in life. That's when he or she begins to acquire distance; in trying to bridge the gap that's developed, contact is initiated. Contact isn't static human co-existence, it's imitation, play, breathing in and out in the broadest sense, being first together with others and then self-contained and alone. Autistic children are all tangled up in the Nessus shirt the world provides and don't dare free themselves. The world casts a spell on them because they haven't taken the step of discrimination, of recognizing things for what they are. For instance, they might pick up a book and just run their fingers along the edges because they haven't grasped that it's a book that can be opened and shut. They haven't come into connection with it as egos, but live in the object itself to such an extent that they can't comprehend it.[6]

At this stage of development something begins to happen—or at least should happen—that is the only right way to develop distance, and that's the awakening of language.

Once language has begun to develop, World, Body, and Ego come together to form the triangle (please don't take that mystically) that is our home base for making contact with others. I'll talk about how and in what form that comes about in a later lecture. In order to really understand it, we'll have to look first at the problem of right and left, which is our topic for tomorrow.

4. The Problem of Right and Left

Today we must attempt another stage of the journey we've undertaken, and with today's subject, "The Problem of Right and Left," we enter another extraordinarily varied landscape. Time will not permit us to travel through this landscape from one end to the other, but it should at least be possible for us to get a panoramic view of it.

Before we do that, however, let's look back at the scenery we surveyed yesterday in attempting to describe the dual process of becoming human. On the one hand, we described the step leading to taking hold of one's own physical body and called it incarnation. At the same time, and fully integrated into this process, another step, which we called discrimination is taking place—stepping into the world and into the possibility of gradually differentiating among the phenomena we meet out there.

I tried to point out how the world is a single unified experience for a baby, and that taking the steps from infancy to being a pre-schooler to being a child of school age means that individual things, forms, objects, colors, and beings begin to be distinguishable and stand out in this general experience. If you find the word "discrimination" too complicated, we can replace it with the word "analysis." We experience the world by becoming aware of it "analytically," step by step. Our experience of our own body is just the opposite, only becoming a totality step by step as we gradually acquire something that is increasingly recognized by modern neurology and known as body image. This is a synthesizing process.

Thus, incarnation is the path leading to the synthesis of our own bodily nature, while the path leading to discrimination in the world is an analytical one. Let's keep in mind the words "analysis" and "synthesis" in relationship to the outer world and the physical body, because we'll need to be thoroughly aware of this duality and call it to mind again later on when we speak about the development of the human form.

Now let's go one step further, taking the "compass" we acquired yesterday and using it to explore the landscape of right and left. The problems we encounter include twinning, cleft formations, and hemiplegia, and many more could be added to the list of what we'll meet in this landscape. Our compass, however, consists of the trinity we used in understanding the stages of incarnation, namely, the trinity of focusing, grasping, and stepping. When we point them out, of course, it's obvious that we're not simply naming three activities. We're proceeding from the top to the middle to the bottom of the human organism, just as a baby proceeds through three steps of incarnation in the first year of life in learning to focus, to grasp, and to take steps.

Now let's try to relate this trinity to the three-dimensional experience of space we've already mentioned briefly. Last time, we asked what it means if we say that a quadriplegic is not active enough in the relationship between forward and back, that a paraplegic has a disturbance in the relationship between up and down, and a hemiplegic in the relationship between right and left. Let's take a closer look at this.

Nowadays people talk a lot about depth psychology but have no idea how superficial this psychology actually is. It hasn't really reached down into the depths at all yet—such as the depths of the four lowest senses mentioned in passing last night, or the depths of three-dimensionality we're concerned with now. It will only really become an "in-depth" psychology when it can illuminate our experience of our physical body so that we can really know the truth of what's going on in these depths. When we speak of the psychology of the subconscious and simply mean instincts, factor analysis, and things like that, that's still all on the surface of our soul-life—though we can be grateful, at least, that this so-called depth psychology has replaced a still more superficial psychology of consciousness. But it's not really a psychology of the subconscious at all yet, and only begins to become one when, for example, we as budding curative educators begin to experience the following.

We took the trinity of focusing, grasping, and stepping as our starting point. If, when you look, you simply gaze, you experience a two-dimensional image spread out in a single plane in front of you, parallel to your forehead and to the frontal plane of your body (Figure 1). Our seeing takes place in this plane to begin with, but something else must be added to it. When focusing on an object, we try not only to gaze in the frontal plane but also to make the axes of our eyes cross so we see the object. The sound "ee" in "see" tells us something of the character of this activity.[1] When we focus on something, we step out of the frontal plane and enter into an experience of depth; the object or being or whatever it is, is grasped not only on a surface but also in its position in depth on the sagittal plane, which is the one dividing right and left (Figure 1). Let's agree to put it like this, quite simply, so that we understand each other: seeing in one plane (gazing) becomes seeing in two planes (focusing), and this experience of going from gaze to focus is not simply the means of perceiving objects. It also contains something that gives us a dull, semi-conscious ego-awareness, grasped through focusing, in the act of separating "here" and "there." For the time being, we must hold on to the fact that we break through the frontal plane with our eyes and pass through it into the experience of depth when we focus.

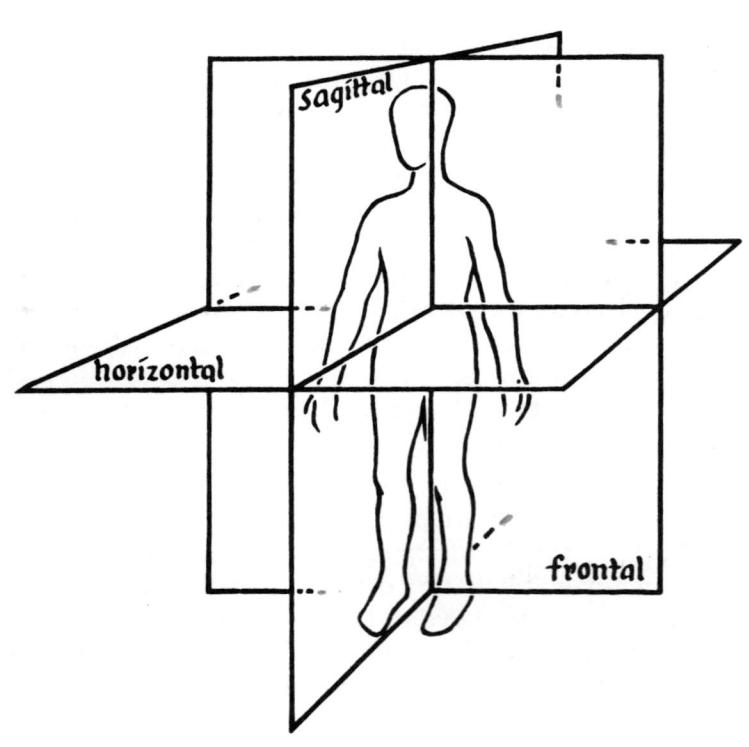

Figure 1.

The next step is grasping. You see, when we want to orient ourselves in reference to our arms and chest, we're in a different plane. Now try to take the very first step in experiencing your Self and your bodily nature, for instance, by consciously following your breath in inhaling and exhaling, and notice how your arms, from this point of view, are hardly anything more than an extension of the whole breathing process. This is nothing new, but it is essential. The arms are also breathing organs, because in birds, for instance, they are transformed into wings, which then "breathe" in the world, i.e., fly. Flying is a breathing process! And you only need to take a pair of ribs and open it up gently to make it metamorphose into a right and a left arm. The plane in which inhaling and exhaling take place is the horizontal plane, and the orientation of human beings in their middle organization, where they breathe and use their hands and arms, is in this plane between up and down. Someone who grasps, whether in touching him or herself by bringing right and left hands together or in grasping an object, is led out of this plane between up and down into the sagittal plane we've already encountered.

First let's look at the crossing of the ocular axes (Figure 2)—when they cross, we focus. Now let's look at the arms and hands coming together, but not crossing, in order to grasp. And when we go one step further down, to stepping, you'll notice right away that the feet and legs don't even touch each other, but are parallel. But not only that, they also have to extend in front or in back of the frontal plane, and above and below the horizontal plane. So we have the sagittal plane linked with the frontal (focus), the sagittal with the horizontal (grasp), and all three together—sagittal, frontal, and horizontal (step). The result is nothing less than the vertical line of our ego-experience. This line lies in the sagittal plane separating right and left and runs through our entire organism and our entire existence. Only when it is constantly experienced in focusing, grasping, and stepping do I experience myself as an individuality. That's a bit of depth psychology that really shouldn't be forgotten.

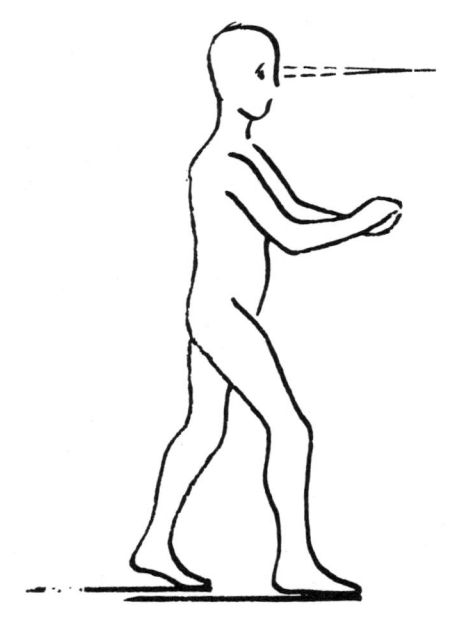

Figure 2.

Now let's go on and take a look at the quadriplegic and the hemiplegic. How do quadriplegic children who are paralyzed in all four limbs experience life? Their paralysis lies in the frontal plane, as we begin to know—in the plane where the world appears to us as two-dimensional as we gaze. Quadriplegic children, the lonely individuals, as we called them, live in what's in front, in the day, so to speak. But what's in back is dark, unknown, and cut off, and gives rise to anxiety. These children are full of anxiety—and then they smile in an attempt to overcome it. What they need to learn is to look, to focus, in order to get out of this two-dimensionality that sees only the day and has an infinite fear of darkness and night. You have to practice with them so you can lay them down on their backs without having them start to scream, because they haven't penetrated and organized their backs properly yet. You'll know what I mean if I say they're too little aware of their backs through the senses of life and self-movement. Their entire experience is of the front, of the upper surface of existence. Everything belonging to the experience of what's behind or to the interplay between forward and back, such as the curative eurythmy gestures for "no" and "yes," isn't there at all yet. That's the quadriplegic.

If you look at paraplegics, you'll see that they're quite free in the upper half; they're alive in their arms and can move their heads freely. They are oriented upward, toward buoyancy, and are totally lacking in gravity, heaviness, or rootedness in the earth. Now you know why children like this seem to drift away from you constantly, wrapping themselves up in wonderful clever ideas, but never taking hold of the earth or of darkness, never penetrating gravity. They need curative-educational treatment in order to acquire uprightness as an inner experience. Now you can see the idea begin to come to life that front and back, right and left, up and down aren't always interchangeable in space as they must be in mathematics and geometry. For someone who studies the human being, front and back separate two worlds we can call day and night. Up and down are two totally different worlds that we can call lightness and heaviness or buoyancy and gravity. These things are of the greatest importance. Not that you have to memorize them, but you should begin to experience that day is here and night there; that lightness is up here and heaviness down there; that lightness is actually morning and heaviness evening. That's why you feel tired and "heavy" in the evening, and light, "on top of things," even a bit "high" in the morning if you've slept well. These are not merely labels—they come out of direct experiences that have simply grown very dull in us modern human beings. We must engender them anew in ourselves so that we can understand it when a child is heavy, or constantly skips away, or only takes things in by looking at them like a deaf person, or can't experience the night like the quadriplegic. It all depends on being able to recreate and re-enliven these things in ourselves.

Finally, let's take a look at the hemiplegic. (Cleft-formations and twins fall into the same category, as we'll see later on.) Hemiplegics are simply human beings who can't experience this ego-line as directly and immediately as those whose right and left sides are harmoniously formed and working together within their bodily organization.

I want to give you an example to show just how deeply this all penetrates our existence, but unfortunately, it only really works in German. When I say the word "I," it always resounds in the frontal plane, which divides consciousness from unconsciousness and day from night. If, however, I say the German word *mir*, meaning "me" or "to me" as in "something happened to me," then it comes about somewhere near the horizontal plane separating up and down. And if I say *mich*, "me" in the sense of "myself" as in "I touch myself" or "I understand myself," then that's down there where stepping, striding, and walking take place. The whole world is included implicitly when the word "I" resounds, because I differentiate between "me" (*mir*) and any other "me". On the other hand, when I say "myself" (*mich*) then I'm only referring to my own ego—my*self*. Being able to say and comprehend I/me/myself means being able to unite right and left intuitively.

Aside from the experience of "me" and "myself," what's the difference between this sagittal plane passing right through us, and the other two planes? The difference is quite obvious. If you look at it, it's not at all difficult to recognize that up and down means head and body. There's such a great difference that the two are polar opposites. And if you look at front and back, "front" is obviously totally different from "back." Face, chest, abdomen, and everything else facing forward make up a totally different world from the unity and pulled-togetherness of the back. You're forced to experience how up and down, front and back are present as complete polarities, disparate right down into their morphology. But right and left are extraordinarily similar. I said "similar"— they are by no means identical. Here we encounter a very specific problem we circumscribe with the simple word "symmetry." We have two hands with five fingers each—they're similar, yet so different that we can never neatly fit one on top of the other. It's impossible, because they belong to two different sides. They're the same and yet different—one right and one left.

When Goethe wrote the story of his life, he called it *Poetry and Truth*, and Eichendorff wrote a novel called *Ahnung und Gegenwart* ("Presentiment and Present").[2] If I write down "poetry" and "truth," and under them "dream" and "reality," then it begins to suggest something intimately related to what right and left actually signify.

Truth/present/reality and poetry/presentiment/dream are the two sides that are similar and yet so different, so totally disparate. These right and left sides present a strange and noteworthy phenomenon; they conceal a lot more than we can grasp immediately.

In the past fifty or sixty years, biologists have performed thousands of experiments in dividing some kind of a fertilized egg, say a newt's or frog's or salamander's egg with a very fine thread. It won't work with the egg of a bird or a mammal, but if the animal is on a more primitive level, instead of each half of the egg simply developing into the right or left half of a single animal, you'll get two lively little frogs or salamanders. The two will be smaller than usual, but they'll be twins. But it's also possible to leave the two halves just barely connected in the middle, instead of dividing the egg completely. What happens then? In that case, it develops into one newt on the right and another on the left, but they're grown together in the middle like Siamese twins, with only four legs between them, two right and two left, and only one tail. You can carry it still further, so that you almost get a single newt, but it has two mouths and two tips on its tail, and still only four legs. Do you see what I'm getting at?

Even with human beings, there are uniovular (identical) and biovular (fraternal) twins, and Siamese twins as well. Very thorough investigations have been made of identical twins. I'm going to quote results of studies published in the 1940s by Roman-Goldzieher. What he found out was a real slap in the face for heredity researchers, who still haven't recovered. In 73% of all cases of identical twins, one twin is left-handed and the other right-handed; that is, nearly three quarters of them belong together. But if you take fraternal twins instead of identical twins and examine the right/left polarity, you'll find that only 60% of fraternal twins are like that, with one of each, and the rest, about 22% and 19% are either both right-handed or both left-handed. What does that mean? It means that fraternal twins are much further along on the path toward individualization than identical twins.

When you're done looking at that, we can turn to another chapter in the problem of right and left.

I've seen a whole series of very handicapped and difficult children, probably between twenty and thirty of them, with all kinds of previous diagnoses. It was quite obvious that these children were double formations—they looked as if they were single entities, but they actually consisted of a right and a left with a morphological (though not visible) gap remaining between them. Thus, for instance, one boy was able to move his right and left sides quite naturally, but the psychological relationship between right and left, what I called "experiencing myself" (*mich*) was insufficiently developed. I remember one girl in Scotland whose eyes were set so far to the sides that she never managed to focus. Grasping was also difficult for her and her walking was uncoordinated. She was one person, but one person with two bodies. Something like these cleft-formations also occurs in a pathological and intensified form (if I may put it like that) in hemiplegia, where one side, either the right or the left, is paralyzed and the other isn't, causing a discrepancy between right and left and disturbing the interplay between them. I already said that this interplay is present right down into the depths of human existence.

What we've talked about so far has very little to do with what we usually call right or left-handedness in a child. That's only the basis for what we'll talk about now, a new problem we'll have to describe with another new word, I'm afraid. If you want to understand what's really involved in the question of right or left-handedness, we have to add the word "dominance"—whether a person's right or left side is dominant. Most of us are born with both a right and left side; we all consist of dream and daytime, fantasy and fact, presentiment and the present. This is the prerequisite for the development of dominance after the third year of life. It seldom happens earlier, because in a baby the two sides are usually balanced out and used more or less interchangeably. Dominance is basically nothing more than the development of an orientation toward the upper right front in focusing and grasping.

Dominance is necessary if a child is to develop distance, an idea we came up with already yesterday.[3] As this distance from one's surroundings comes about, the process of analyzing the world and the synthesis of one's bodily nature begin to work together. But not all children develop this possibility. You mustn't imagine that right-handedness is the general rule. Statistics over the past twenty years tell us something quite different. About 51% of all people are fully right-sided, which means that the right eye leads in focusing, the right hand in grasping, and the right foot in walking—in other words, focusing, grasping, and stepping are all oriented toward the right. About 4% are fully left-sided, with focusing, grasping, and stepping all directed to the left.[4] The rest are the ones who always give us the greatest difficulty in school, at home, and in counseling services—the 45% who can't decide whether to be right-sided or left-sided, but are right-eyed, left-handed, and left-footed, for example, or left-eyed, right-handed, and left-footed. There are any number of possible combinations. But these children (who write right-handed but follow what they've written with the left eye, for instance) are the ones who most often cause trouble in class, often reacting neurotically or even psychopathically to their own lack of orientation. We won't talk about assessment methods now. But one thing still needs to be said, and that is the following:

Immeasurable suffering and improper treatment has been caused by the proliferation of a school of thought originating in America at the beginning of this century claiming, "Right-handed is good; left-handed's not bad. If we train both, we'll develop both sides of the brain and create superhumans." Are you aware that this got as far as German remedial schools in the first decade of this century? That children were forced to learn to write with both hands? Then of course, people took steps against it. Rudolf Steiner himself warned again and again of the dangers of training children to be ambidextrous.

Making a left-sided child switch over to the right is a criminal act no teacher should be permitted anymore, because it interferes negatively in the whole development and destiny of the child. Of course, you can continue to attempt to orient the 45% who are not decidedly either right or left-handed to the right side as a matter of course, because if you do, you pull them out of their instability and bring about a certain consistent direction in their existence, whether they were left-handed, right-eyed, and right-footed, or whatever. But it simply should not happen that a person who's come to earth as a left-sided human being and is supposed to go through life like that (I leave it up to you whether you want to call it destiny or something else) is suddenly forced to change direction. Of course, destiny can intervene, if, for instance, a child born to be left-sided has an accident and her left side is paralyzed. Then of course she has to switch over to the right altogether, since she can't write with her left hand anymore. The torment and difficulties this causes have to be overcome in a case like this, painful as it may be.[5]

So, have you understood that the problem of dominance is something different from the problem of right and left? Don't get them mixed up. A cow or any other animal also has right and left legs, and even a baby, although it has no dominance as yet, has a right and a left side. Dominance comes about out of the experience of "I" and "myself" that makes us whole human beings through the relationship of presentiment to present, fantasy to fact. (It only came about gradually in the course of the cultural epochs, too, by the way. We could talk about that for a long time.) The development of an orientation toward the upper right front makes possible not simply the experience of one's ego (which is there already), but clear, strong, ego-permeated day-consciousness; this, however, necessarily includes everything we carry in us from "behind," as beings of the night, as well as from "in front," as beings of the day. Each of us consists of a day person and a night person put together; it's just that the day person in someone right-sided is oriented toward the front and the night person toward the back.

5. The World of Language

Karl König begins this lecture by reviewing what he said about symmetry and dominance in the previous one, showing how the phenomenon of physical dominance gives rise to the possibility of "distancing" oneself from the world psychologically and is ultimately recognizable as the capacity for self-awareness on a spiritual level.[1] Then he continues:

Now, all the things I tried to indicate so briefly are very directly and intimately bound up with the world of language, which we'll try to talk about a bit today. Only a speaking person is truly a human being. That doesn't mean that someone who remains mute because of some injury or retardation isn't also a human being, for each individual carries within him or herself the potential for speech just by virtue of being human, so to speak, so it's valid to say that only a speaking human being is truly human.

This is better known nowadays than we usually assume, because really progressive anthropologists, special educators, and neurologists and psychiatrists know perfectly well that speech is something quite extraordinary. In his special-education text, Asperger says that cultivated speech is the "noblest and highest expression of the human soul and spirit."[2] It would hardly be possible to put it any better than that. But language and speaking are achievements that can hardly be compared to any other human ability or attribute. Whenever a human being speaks, a seed of something new in his or her life begins to unfold. The language we speak—if I may put it like that—is the birth of a second human being in each of us. That's how complete and perfect an entity language is in itself, language and everything leading to communication and mutual understanding.

Simply describing it like that, however, is not enough. Next we have to begin to imagine what's actually happening when a person speaks, because unless we first acquire some basic concepts about that, we can't possibly come to an understanding of abnormalities in speaking and language learning. People speak. But they can only do so if two things come together in them—language itself, on the one hand, and speaking on the other. We must have language in order to be able to speak, and we must be able to speak in order to express ourselves through language. Language and speaking are two totally different determining factors. A human being who has language but can't speak will only get as far as babbling. In spite of "having language," for instance, infants who haven't learned to speak and articulate, but have already begun to perceive a bit of language, can't speak because their speech organs aren't able to express themselves yet. Equally, people who have no language because of being unable to hear or understand the spoken word, also can't speak. They'll try anything in order to be able to articulate, but language eludes them. We can only talk about the speaking human being when language (as an entity independent of speaking) and speaking (as a motor achievement) come together.

Now let's try to look back at some of the things we talked about earlier. You'll recall that we talked about how a child learns to speak through being able to walk and to think by being able to speak. In this context, we talked about "incarnation" as the process of taking possession of our physical nature. But incarnation isn't the only step in child development—there's also the process of taking hold of the world, which we called "discrimination." I've already pointed out that discrimination is just as important as incarnation, especially with regard to speech. Just as discrimination is the polar opposite of incarnation, hearing is the polar opposite of walking. We become conscious of language through hearing just as we learn to speak through walking. Through the combination of language and speaking, human beings begin to talk. By way of hearing and language (not *speaking*), the discrimination we talked about can begin to develop. As I said before, the moment we begin to name things, the world around us wakes up, and we become conscious of the world, just as incarnation makes us aware of our body. Thinking can develop only when speaking and language come together later on. (Figure 1)

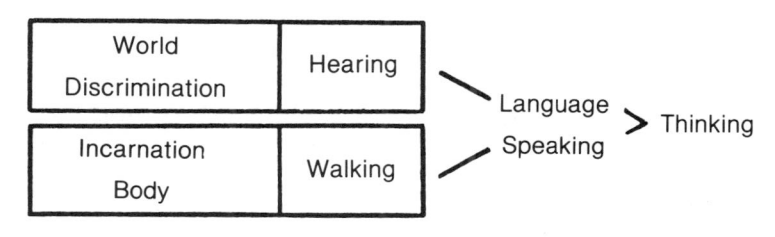

World Discrimination	Hearing	⟶ Language ⟶	Thinking
Incarnation Body	Walking	⟶ Speaking ⟶	

Figure 1.

At this point, I'd like to draw your attention to the fact that when we consider the speaking human being, we always need to be aware that both motor (expressive) and sensory (perceptive) components are involved. Instead of "motor" and "sensory" I could also say "body and world" or "incarnation and discrimination," but in any case, these two components work together more intimately in speech than anywhere else. Indeed, that's what's so wonderful about human speech, that world and body, sensory and motor systems, flow together in such a way that one could scarcely exist without the other anymore. If you want, you can say that language is the soul of the person speaking. You could also say that speaking is the body of language. Now you'll understand why I said that whenever a human being begins to speak, an inner seed begins to germinate into something effectively that person's equal. Language is the microcosm in the cosmos of the human being. It's certainly not the case, however, that people who can speak and have language have reached the culmination of these possibilities—namely, that they can account for themselves and answer freely. When children who are one year old or a bit older learn to speak and put their first words together, they can only really do it right if a third prerequisite is present in addition to the two we mentioned earlier. I'll read you a passage from Asperger's text again. He says, "Understanding the objective content of what is spoken, the sense of word, is acquired earlier than one's own ability to speak." We can observe how developing children usually understand more words than they can say. That's the case with almost everyone, by the way. As a general rule, we all understand more than we can say. The people who say more than they can understand are a notable exception. All things being equal, however, we're usually like children in that we understand more than we can say. So *understanding* is the third prerequisite. As soon as we say that, we confront one of the greatest philosophical, anthropological, and special-educational problems in existence.

How is it possible that a small child who has just learned to stand, who has as yet no ability to form concepts, let alone think, can nonetheless understand spoken words? Where does this come from? Just imagine what a monumental problem this is. Years ago, Rudolf Steiner already pointed out something essential in this regard, and even if he'd done nothing else, that would have been reason enough to include him among the most important philosophers of our century. He pointed out that just as there are senses of smell, hearing, sight, and taste, a "sense of word" exists, as well as a still higher sense he called "sense of thought." These must be duly emphasized, for without them we would not be able to understand the spoken word at all. But what does this all mean? We must begin to deal with these two senses seriously and wrestle with them just as the philosopher Husserl and his pupil Scheler did, who were on the verge of recognizing that the sense of word exists. Rudolf Steiner, on the other hand, described it clearly and unmistakably as a sense through which, instead of perceiving colors, smells, tastes, lines, forms, or warmth, we recognize spoken language as such.

As curative educators, we are confronted with the following enigma again and again: We meet children who can hear, whose sense of hearing for sounds, tones, and noises in general is perfectly intact, but they still can't distinguish the spoken word from anything else they hear. They don't even notice that people who are speaking use their lips, teeth, tongue, mouth, and cheeks to project speech out into the world, because in these children that heightening of the sense of hearing, the sense of word, could not develop. There would be much to say on that subject. But we're also often confronted with a different problem: It's possible for certain children or adults to be able to tell whether someone's just going "ba ba ba" or saying actual words, such as "Come on, go into the woods." And yet "Come on, go into the woods" remains a mere sequence of sounds for them and doesn't become a meaningful content. In a case like this, the next higher sense, the sense of thought, is either incompletely developed or wholly undeveloped. We must recognize this as a further basis for understanding the whole problem of language. I know it's terribly difficult to learn to think a new thought like this, but just try to follow it. We must put it like this: Through hearing, we perceive noises or tones in general. The sense of word transmits an infinite variety of sounds, all kinds of combinations of vowels and consonants, which become words, but if we had only this sense for speech sounds or "sense of word," we still wouldn't be able to understand the content of speech. It would be as if people were addressing us in a foreign language. Only when the sense of thought is added are words and sentences perceived in such a way that ideas can unfold in them.

That's why there are centers for speaking and understanding in the brain where impressions of the sense of word are processed just as visual impressions are processed in the center for sight. Understanding speech is not a question of decoding or analyzing or thinking about a series of ciphers present in speech. It's a matter of direct perception, just as color is a matter of direct perception for the sense of sight. The spoken word is perceived as such by the sense of word, and the meaning or communication in it, contained in words and sounds, is perceived by the listener's sense of thought. We can truly enter into the sphere of language only once we really begin to take these senses into account. And it's only because we all carry the senses of word and thought within us that conversation, which Goethe calls "more precious than gold," is possible.

We might summarize this by saying that the motor component (speaking) comes from below while the sensory component (language) comes from above. The sense of hearing, through which the tonal character of speaking is revealed to us, the sense of word, through which sounds are recognized as speech sounds, and the sense of thought, which lifts speech sounds up into meaning, are all at work in this sensory component of speech. Now we need to take the analysis of these things a bit further.

Something fundamental always gets overlooked in ordinary textbooks' discussions of speech and language disorders and the mysteries of sounds and speech sounds, namely the fact that people speak! Many people nowadays already know that speech consists of the two components I described in the beginning—that is, of language and of speaking as a motor activity. Many also begin to recognize that a third factor, *understanding* the spoken word, needs to be added. But what they still overlook is the fact that we have to be able to hear what we're saying ourselves as we say it. Speaking requires an incredible effort if you can't hear what you're saying. Deaf or hearing impaired people have trouble with speech not only because they can't hear what others say, but also because they can't hear themselves speak. Being deaf means primarily not being able to perceive one's own speech. What makes a deaf person's speech harsh and poorly articulated, with no melody or flow, is the fact that this interplay between expressive and receptive speech is disturbed.

If someone could examine your larynx with a sufficiently fine mirror or some kind of resonating device right now while you're listening to me speak, you'd find out that it's vibrating silently along with my words, without any conscious intent on your part. That means that while I'm speaking, I hear myself and so do other people, but they're not just listening, they're also speaking silently along with me. Understanding via the melody and rhythm of sentence structures can only be complete because of this intermingling of sensory and motor components, of receptive and expressive language. Perhaps this diagram will help us in our curative-educational attempts to understand speech abnormalities. (Figure 2)

I've just described spoken language. Perhaps we can indicate it with a figure like this. (A) But heard language, receptive language, sinks down into this expressive speech. (B) The two cross over into each other. You only need to draw a suggestion of ears here and of a mouth and larynx there, and you'll notice how the one actually passes over into the other. Tones stream in through the ear and become speech sounds, words, and ideas by virtue of the fact that we have the senses of hearing, word, and thought up here. (B) This is the area of receptive language.

Down below we have motor activity working upwards from the limbs, turning into gestures that accompany speech and enhance and support it and streaming upward into the larynx. And what happens in the larynx? Motor activity, with the help of the flow of exhaled air, is transformed into speech sounds. Do you remember how I told you on our second evening, when we were talking about motor activity, that all movement is actually music or sound? In the larynx the flow of motor activity comes to a halt and is transformed so that sound is born out of movement. The organs of speech—teeth, tongue, lips, palate, and cheeks—take this sound and transform it into the different vowels and consonants. This is the motor activity of speaking. Language, comprehension, the perceived word or sound, sinks down into it, and then the melodic line of a sentence comes about. This already carries meaning, because you express some things in iambic rhythms and others in trochaic, and if you say *"I'm going"* that's something totally different from *"I'm going"* or *"I'm going."* This is only possible because the whole person speaks, because everything you are as a human being pours into your receptive and

Language
Sense of Thought

Sense of Word Hearing

B

Ear　　　　　Ear

Mouth
Larynx　　　Understood　Language

Motor Activity
of Speaking

A

Gestures

Motor Activity

Receptive

Expressive

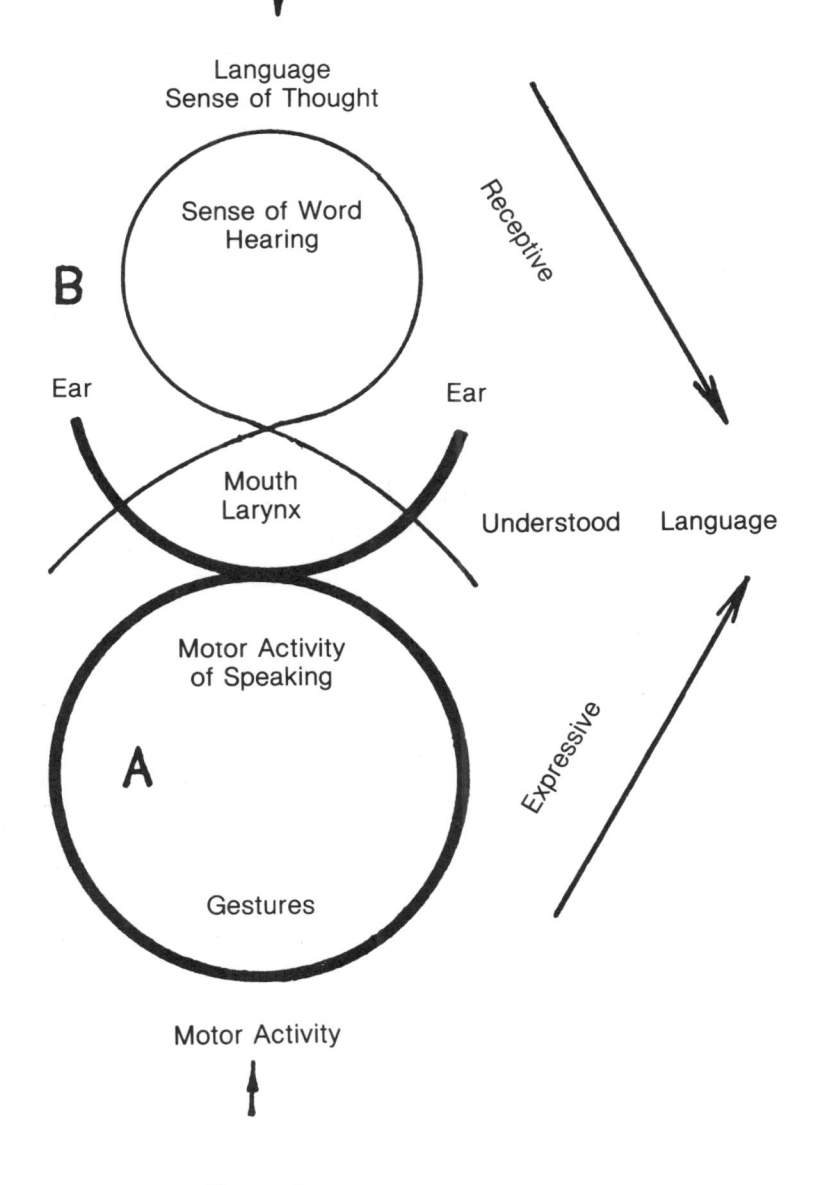

Figure 2.

expressive speech. Speech is not merely an ability to be acquired like any other, though it's also that, to some slight extent. It's also not merely a means of communication, to be replaced by some other means if need be. Speech, like movement, is first and foremost a way for a human individuality to make itself known and reveal the inner world of the person in question.

You see, when we talk to each other and encounter each other in speaking, it's as if your speech opens an eye through which I can look into your inner being, into your experience, thinking, perception, and feelings. It's one of the most important exercises for budding curative educators to listen to the speech of the children in their care—not to just listen in order to understand what they mean, since that's often totally incomprehensible, but to listen to how they speak, and thus to experience something of their more intimate nature. That's what's important.

Modern philosophers have a rough time with the problem of language because someone like Wittgenstein totally denies any inner communication through speech—as far as he's concerned, the possibility doesn't even exist.[3] We are all lonely because language is simply a means of communication we've acquired and agreed upon, but it doesn't convey what the other person is feeling at all. The polar opposite of this point of view is the kind of ingenious and exaggerated living into language that somebody like Heidegger does, which leads to a total individualization of language. We must not deny that language is an expression of cosmic occurrences, that the nature of a head is contained in the very word "head," and that a tree is contained in the word *"Baum"* for Germans, in the word *"arbre"* for the French, and in the word "tree" for the English. The difference is that the English-speaking person is looking at the trunk—

"tree"—the German at the crown—"*Baum,*"—and the French speaker at the branches and twigs, which are called "*arbre.*" As long as we won't admit this and go on believing that our great-great-grandmothers got together when they were still apes and agreed to call a tree "tree," we'll never come to any understanding of what language truly is.

Excuse me for putting it so crudely, but most current theories on the evolution of language are like that, claiming that it developed out of barking and meowing and so on, because people don't have the slightest idea that each thing and being bears its own name within it. Human speech reveals the names, and that's why communication and (to take it one step further) true understanding are altogether possible. That's what we need as a basis for understanding the nature of speech and language disorders.

Basically, there's no such thing as a child in need of curative-educational treatment who doesn't have some kind of speech disturbance. Speech disorders are not always separate phenomena appearing in the same way disturbances in movement or thinking do. Children with greater or lesser difficulties make themselves known through speech just like any other human beings. When we approach a child with the intention of analyzing his or her speech, we must do it from two sides right from the beginning. We have to ask how much of the disorder comes from the motor or expressive side and how much from the sensory or receptive side. There are very few cases of pure motor-disturbance in speech. I'll just mention a few in passing. Stammering and stuttering are both purely motor disturbances, even though they often have an emotional basis, and if you see people stuttering, you'll notice the movement disturbance in their speech musculature right away. Rare forms of "motor aphasia" also belong in this category. These people have no possibility to form speech sounds at all.

Then there are the many varied forms of sensory-motor disturbances—not pure motor disturbances, but sensory-motor speech disorders. The first is the disturbance due to deafness or hearing impairment. Next there's the type I already mentioned, in which hearing is present but the sense of word is impaired. We call that "sensory aphasia." That means that a child with this condition does hear, certainly, but can't clearly distinguish noises and tones from actual speech sounds. And then there's something called "agnostic aphasia" or "psychological deafness" in which the person hears what someone else is saying and recognizes it as speech, as the spoken word, but still has the greatest difficulties understanding what's being said. A lot could be said about these three, because all of them—the deaf-mute, the aphasic, and the agnostic aphasic—also always have motor difficulties in speaking. Motor and sensory factors are all mixed up together.

Really purely sensory disorders in which people speak little or not at all are almost always psychological in origin. For instance, the main reason autistic children don't speak is because they're so caught up in the world (as I described before) that they haven't acquired the distance needed to separate the thing from the word, the object from its name. You'll also find a whole group of profoundly retarded people, imbeciles, if I may put it like that, who never wake up in the sphere of the senses of word and thought at all, but are trapped at the level of hearing. The motor system of these people remains very primitive as well—for instance, the individualization of the voluntary muscular system scarcely takes place. It's justified to call this purely sensory aphasia even though the motor system of speech hasn't been developed. You'll also find a large number of children who voluntarily reject the use of the word because of negativistic traits brought on by experiences of shock, rejection, or misunderstanding on the part of the world around them. If you observe them while they're sleeping and dreaming, you'll notice that they really can and do speak, although they refuse to when conscious.

These are only brief indications of all that could be said. I'd actually have to go on to speak in detail about spastics, athetotics, children with Down's syndrome, and so on, which would take us ever deeper into the great and all-embracing world of language. I do still need to mention one thing, however, regarding reading and writing.

In everything we've said about language so far, we've always stayed within the realm of hearing, but language is broader than that. Please note that it doesn't stay confined to hearing. As soon as expressive language leaves the realm of the spoken word and enters into the realm of sight, it is transformed into writing by means of the hand. And when receptive language enters into the world of light, it becomes reading, by means of the eye. This is of fundamental importance. As long as we're only speaking and stay within the realm of the spoken word, the senses of word and thought remain confined to hearing. But when gestures are also perceived and writing develops out of gestures, when speech is transformed into writing, then language enters the world of seeing and light. *All disturbances in reading and writing stem from the fact that the translation or bridge between hearing and seeing is possible only in some partial and fragmented way, or perhaps not at all.*

For instance, children like this can understand wonderfully what's said to them, but what they hear and what they see stay in two separate and distinct regions.

Everything depends on the bridge-building that allows them to understand that a written word is the same as the word they hear, or vice versa. We must become more and more conscious of the fact that all of our pedagogical and curative-educational efforts are directed at connecting one shore with the other, at connecting what is heard with what is seen. Receptive and expressive speech, non-spatial to begin with, have to take on a spatial character and sequence in the realm of seeing and light when we write and read.

If you observe how human beings stand with one foot in the world of hearing and the other in the world of sight, with language and writing connecting them, then you'll be able to realize the great importance of dominance, of the upper/right/front, for eye-hand coordination. It is this dominance that transforms the spoken word into written and readable words. Human beings who read and write step out of the soul-realm of speaking into the spirit-realm of the light. Now you'll understand the difficulties people without a definite one-sided dominance face in trying, for example, to read left-eyed and write right-handed. Reading and writing go their separate ways for people like that. These are all things for which we must try to acquire an ever greater understanding through inner work.

6. The *Gestalt* of the Child

And now, ladies and gentlemen, we come to the end of this course. I've made an attempt—in a more or less aphoristic way, I realize—to give a preliminary outline of diagnosis in curative education. It was nothing more than a beginning, and an incomplete beginning at that, to which we would have to add, for instance, the different forms of seizures occurring during childhood and everything that seizures imply. Perhaps we can do that another time. We would also have to add an entire group of syndromes which have to do with disturbances in the diencephalon and mesencephalon—something I usually call the "thalamus syndrome." Post-encephalitic conditions belong to it, as do infantile autism, the behavioral patterns of childhood schizophrenia, and much of what we usually call hysteria. Retardation caused by metabolic disturbances would also need a lecture for itself; we would need to present in detail, for instance, what phenylketonuria is, or what it means to be an albino. After all that, we would still need to go into the different forms of social maladjustment, neuroses, and psychotic conditions. These would be chapters on their own, too, and I couldn't even take them into account now while we were looking at diagnostics for the first time. I felt it was more important to describe deviations from the archetypal patterns of human growth and development, both incomplete and exaggerated forms of abnormality with their onset in early childhood or even during the embryonic period.

I hope we've all become sensitive to something I

pointed out in our very first meeting—namely that spasticity, a speech disturbance, or any other form of developmental delay is nothing abnormal or pathological in itself, it's simply a condition that takes over in the wrong place at the wrong time. Do you understand now what I mean by that? A spastic has simply remained an undeveloped infant as far as motor development is concerned, an athetotic is simply a very small child who hasn't learned to control his or her movements yet. Of course this becomes pathological if it lasts into the second or third year of life. It's the same with speech disturbances and with all the other conditions we considered. We must recognize ourselves in everything we meet in handicapped children. They simply present us with phenomena that have overshot the mark or have gotten stuck or out of balance.

That's why I think we should still take the time this evening to look at one last thing—namely, at how the *Gestalt* of the child develops. It's not simply a question of morphology, because a person's character and distinctive psychological qualities and peculiarities are revealed through his or her *Gestalt* or physique. We've known this ever since Kretschmer published his important book *Constitution and Character* over forty years ago. Discussion and research along these lines have been going on ever since, and by now we know that each constitutional type is indicative of certain character traits. This detailed research was continued in America by Sheldon and in Germany by Konrad, who died so prematurely. An infinite number of findings have been compiled. The fundamental conclusion remains the same—that a person's constitution does give some indication (I'm expressing myself carefully) of his or her character and disposition. We owe this to Kretschmer. Nevertheless, we must recognize clearly that Kretschmer's constitutional types only apply to men. They aren't applicable at all to women and especially not to children and adolescents. People have tried again and again to find out how Kretschmer's three constitutional types, the pyknic, the asthenic, and the athletic, could be applied to children, but it simply doesn't work. If you try to do it, you get all tangled up in opinions with no evidence to support them, so you should be careful not to describe children in these terms. Although I don't want to go into it now, you should also avoid classifying women as pyknic, asthenic, or athletic. They don't fit into these types; they have totally different constitutional attributes.[1] And what happens with children is that they're constantly in a state of constitutional transformation, which makes it impossible to apply these three types to them. It just doesn't work.

There's only one way you can apply them, and I beg you to take even that with a grain of salt. Those of you who know Kretschmer's categories will have an inkling of what I mean when I say that up to the time of the first transformation of physique in the fifth or sixth year, when the large-headed, small-bodied toddler's physique begins to give way to the more harmonious build of the school-child, we might say that children could be called "infantile pyknics," because all their body cavities (skull, chest, and abdomen) are large, while their limbs are small.[2]

That's what children are like during the first seven-year period—sort of *infantile* pyknics. I emphasize "infantile" on purpose, because it can only be compared superficially with the stocky adult pyknic. During the second seven-year period, when children are of school age, their bodies begin to elongate for the first time. Their limbs grow longer and their heads get smaller in proportion to their bodies. They really become fighters or athletes and can do anything they want to with their limbs.

An unbelievable grace flows through their entire motor system. Still taking it with a grain of salt, we might say that children at this stage have infantile *athletic* bodies. And in the third developmental stage, in puberty, when the limbs elongate even more and everything gets stretched out, children or young people become adolescent *asthenics,* so to speak. So you see, we all basically go through these three different types in the course of our childhood and adolescence. Some tend to remain small and retain the large body cavities of infancy for the rest of their lives. Others remain school-children, athletics, and still others continue to carry the major signs of adolescence with them. Looking at it like this makes it possible to see Kretschmer's types in the right light as far as children are concerned. You really won't be able to apply them differently. As curative educators, we should actively avoid applying this constitutional threefoldness to children and adolescents.[3]

It remains for us to find out what in this whole question of constitution is actually typical of childhood, and I believe we already have a significant basis in a distinction Rudolf Steiner presented to teachers from all possible points of view in many pedagogical lectures. He spoke about the large-headed child and the small-headed child. If you say that today, many people will think they can just go around measuring heads with a tape measure. Of course they'll manage to measure children's heads, but they won't be much the wiser for it in terms of being able to tell which ones are large-headed and which small-headed, because it's not the absolute size of the head that's important, but rather the size of the head in relation to the rest of the body. Someone with a big head can be small-headed and someone with a small head can be large-headed, depending on the relative size of the body. Please look at things the way they are in real life.

Usually, unless it's in a poem by Morgenstern or something like that, heads (or knees) don't go rolling around the world on their own but are supported by bodies, and it all depends on what kind of body it is. Of course, it's also possible to measure bodies, and anyone who wants to take the trouble can go ahead, though I'm not sure it will prove terribly conclusive. After all, to repeat myself just one more time, it's the human being who is the measure of all things, and not the tape measure.

But now let's ask ourselves what Rudolf Steiner meant when he talked about small-headed and large-headed children, keeping in mind that constitution, physique, or bodily build points to certain traits of character. Rudolf Steiner said that large-headed children tend toward an embryonic *Gestalt*. You know that in a newborn the head is typically very large in proportion to the rest of the body. This discrepancy is still much more pronounced if you trace it back before birth—an embryo in the third or fourth month of development is half head. That changes in the course of a lifetime, but a large-headed, childlike person still hearkens back to earlier stages of development. You'll always notice that a large-headed child is much more imaginative than most children. A large-headed child tends to be dreamy and can get totally lost in play, and is usually also slightly far-sighted. A large-headed child has a large imagination as well as a large head, and is at home in a large circumference. In terms of something we described before, the large-headed child belongs to the ones who get stuck in the world's generalities. Discrimination is not developed as strongly as it should be in someone of that particular age.[4]

The exact opposite of the large-headed child is the small-headed one, whose head is smaller and more hardened while the rest of the body is larger and stronger. This child gets too involved in the process of incarnation into the body, incarnates strongly and therefore has a very well-developed memory. (These things go together.) You could characterize large-headed and small-headed children by saying the former have a lot of imagination while the latter have a good memory.

If you trace these conditions to the point where they become pathological, you'll find, in the case of large-headedness, that hydrocephaly represents the state of excess. Hydrocephaly is a condition in which the production of cerebrospinal fluid is stepped up to the point where it more or less prevents the development of the brain. What does that mean? Phenomenologically speaking, it simply means that the life-forces inside the head, the fluid-forming forces, are so alive and strong that they overcome the molding, shape-giving force of the nervous system in the brain. You'll find children with heads so large they can't hold them up any more, the weight of the fluid is so great. So they just lie there, because the power of the life-giving water in the brain is so great that their delicate little bodies have no strength left with which to develop.

These are exceptional and extreme conditions, of course, but much of what we find in them is typically present in less exaggerated cases as well. For example, hydrocephalics are people who always tend to observe with their heads, noticing many things others simply overlook. Their tendency to observe, to be onlookers, is much too strong, and they are reluctant to get their fingers dirty with work. They're the ones who always point out what other people haven't done, but it doesn't occur to them that they could do it themselves. They're the ones who say, "I've been watching you for hours and you haven't done a thing—you really are a lazybones!" That's typically hydrocephalic. If you observe them carefully, you'll also notice something else, namely that their powers of conceptualization and possibility to reproduce ideas are exceptionally limited. On the other hand, everything having to do with language is particularly alive in them. All hydrocephalics and large-headed children are quick to learn to speak, and they speak well, in whole and complicated sentences, if the hydrocephaly is not so advanced that it precludes the possibility of speech altogether. There's a true story about a hydrocephalic boy that I've often told as an example. I asked him if he knew what a cat looks like, and he said he did. "Can you draw a cat for me?" "Yes, I can do that." Then I gave him the chalk, and he "drew" me a cat, and it looked like this: CAT. That was the cat, and he really meant it, because the word had taken the place of the image for him. That's something very significant. These people live in the word to a much greater extent than almost anyone else. It's not the world in its forms, but the world in its names which is alive for them. If you really grasp this, you'll have an idea of the behavior characteristic of a hydrocephalic or large-headed person.

The other extreme is represented by microcephalics, who have very small heads but, if they've developed fully, unusually large and powerful bodies. Their bodily nature is deeply bound up with the transformation of the earth. Microcephalics live in memory and in everything that can be perceived and experienced directly. Once again, let me tell you a little story I've told over and over again just because it's so very characteristic. We had a microcephalic like that, with a head you could hardly see and a gigantic body—an extremely good-natured person, though he could also get very angry. Once we saw a wonderful performance of a fairy tale, and in the end a beautiful maiden came out of a golden gate. I asked Anthony how he had liked it and he said, "Fine! Anna came out of the cupboard that's usually in the laundry."

And it was true. He had observed very exactly and completely missed the point. The important thing for him was that Anna had come out of the laundry cupboard. It was beyond his possibilities to see her as a beautiful maiden coming out through a golden gate. That's typically microcephalic.

From this, we can gather that form-giving forces are at work in the head. If they're too weak, the body becomes too large, but if they're too strong, they are restricted to the head and the body remains small. In the first case, memory and concrete understanding are what develop strongly; in the second, imagination is more pronounced. All of us have both hydrocephalic and microcephalic tendencies, only in most of us they're kept in some kind of balance, so that we each have a certain amount of both fantasy and memory. It's only when someone's head gets too large or too small that the conditions described above come about.

If you can empathize with hydrocephalics, feel your way into them, then you'll notice that they're actually people who are always the way you are when you're just waking up. Then you can use your head and your senses already, but actually taking hold of things is still difficult—they tend to just slip out of your hand. That's what hydrocephalics are like all the time. If you feel your way into what it's like to be microcephalic, you'll find it's just how you are in the evening after a hard day's work, when you're tired and scarcely managing to stay awake. Everything becomes difficult; you can still just manage to do a bit of work, but thinking and speaking are almost impossible anymore. If you really take in images like these and apply them in making a curative diagnosis, you'll be able to use them to make some very fundamental observations.

There is still one more thing I have to add. There's a

type of microcephalic who isn't simply microcephalic but also has a very small body. Microcephalics of this type remain underdeveloped and never learn to speak. They have strangely bent noses and hair like a fur cap, which led earlier curative educators to call them the "Aztec type." On the other hand, there's also a type of hydrocephalic who is a really massively built person with a large body as well as a large head. These types point to the giants and dwarfs we know from myths and legends. I'm not saying they actually existed. I'm only pointing out that primal states of human existence break through in human types like these. Let me just indicate the medical-physiological aspect briefly: If the activity of the pineal gland predominates, large-headed or hydrocephalic conditions come about. If the activity of the pituitary gland predominates, this leads to the overdevelopment of the limbs, appendages, and so on. I wanted to point this out because I think it's important for us to consider physical types like these.

You know that in the past hundred years, mongoloid children have begun to appear in great variety. They've appeared all over the world in all shapes and forms and are at home in all races. Negroes and Mongols, Malays, Indians, and Eskimos all have their share of children with Down's syndrome. They are much more numerous than the cretins of 150 or 200 years ago. Now you see, this is another case of a primal state of the human form or *Gestalt* breaking through, because mongolism is nothing more than an incomplete morphological development. Mongoloid children have basically gotten stuck in an earlier morphological stage. That's why Haubold, though from a different point of departure (point of view) , felt it necessary to introduce therapies to help them mature belatedly, therapies which have proved quite helpful, within limits. Children with Down's syndrome can never turn into normal human beings, but at least those who've been treated become able to put up a bit more resistance toward (against) life than those who haven't.

In contrast to that, the cretin is a type we can describe by saying the person hardened much too early. If someone asks us what mongoloids are really like, we can only answer that they're as incomplete and wonderfully childlike in soul and character as they are immature in physique. Cretins are just the opposite. They have fallen away from childishness and imaginative existence too early, and many untreated cretins become hardened and wrapped up in their sexuality.

Let me repeat once again that looking at things like this can provide guiding images for curative diagnostics. We must learn to pay attention to each child's *Gestalt*, to how he or she looks, walks, moves, and carries his or her body. Do you realize that looking at a child's hands is one of the most important observations a teacher can make? Are the fingers still like those of an infant? Are they hyperextensible? Is the hand broad or narrow? Are the fingers permeated by life and blood? Are they ensouled? That is, do you have the feeling that they've already become individualized, or are they still totally unpenetrated by the child's soul? As prospective curative educators, you should get into the habit not only of looking at each of your children's fingers but also of recalling in the evening how these fingers are formed, and whether the child grasps a pen or pencil with three fingers or two—that's much, much more important than an electroencephalogram. You should actually never look at children from a curative-educational point of view without taking off their socks and shoes and seeing how the soles of their feet touch the earth, whether their feet rest flat on the ground or are arched, whether or not the bones in the middle of the foot have broken down so that they're flat-footed. You can tell from the form of the foot whether or not a child is brain-damaged.

When we diagnose from the curative-educational point of view, all our observations should be filled with compassion, for compassion is not just something subjective. If you have compassion for a child with underdeveloped fingers and learn to feel what it's like to have fingers that can't do anything, or to have to write with your right hand while reading with your left eye so that the establishment of dominance and distance becomes incredibly difficult, then you'll know out of empathy what you as a curative educator must do for that child, without having to look it up in a textbook.

What we need in order to come to a curative-educational diagnosis is devotion to details—love for the shape of a nose or the way a lip is chiseled or how someone's teeth are formed. We need to be able to look at these wonders with devotion and with a good dose of compassion—not the kind you drown in, but the kind that can be transformed into deeds of love. When that happens, curative diagnostics comes alive. Then you, as a curative educator, will be able to approach these children and young people by appealing to their eternal individuality. You'll be able to either teach them to live with their disability and accept it positively, or help them overcome it, at least to some extent. But you have to appeal again and again to that immortal individuality which is present in every single child, no matter how ill. And then, in spite of the inadequacy of all we've described, our efforts will be transformed into living activity in each single one, and that's what matters.

PART II

Epilepsy and Hysteria

1. An Introduction to Convulsive Disorders

Our topic for the next three sessions will be a complex of interrelated phenomena which we could entitle "Epilepsy and Hysteria," although we'll be speaking of hysteria not in the usual and current meaning of the word, but in the special way Rudolf Steiner defined it. He spoke of a pair of opposites, a kind of human polarity between epilepsy, broadly defined, on the one hand, and hysteria on the other. Part of what Rudolf Steiner presented in the Curative Course of 1924 will provide the basis for what we will discuss here.

To begin with, however, we will be particularly concerned with "epilepsy" in the broadest sense, although by now it's no longer quite justified to use that word. It's a word in common usage, and of course we can and will continue to use it too. Actually, however, we should learn to avoid the word "epilepsy" because it stigmatizes people who suffer from seizures and may be called epileptics. By now our knowledge of the phenomena of seizures has become so differentiated that, in my opinion, it would be justified to speak only of convulsive seizures of varying kinds and degrees, with or without loss of consciousness. By focusing on this idea of seizures of different kinds and degrees, with or without loss of consciousness, we describe things instead of pinning them down and leave them open instead of defining them.

There are many, many people who suffer from attacks of convulsions now and then without being "epileptics."

Indeed, we must get used to the idea that every human being is capable of having seizures. If I were to exaggerate a bit I could even say that convulsions are an inherent attribute of both human beings and higher animals. There is no human being who would not react to certain extreme circumstances by having a seizure. As soon as we really start looking at this fact, we see the whole thing in a new light. And if we also consider that children, especially infants, are much more seizure-prone than adults, we will come to regard seizure-susceptibility as part of the human condition, just like rage and anxiety, shame and fear, laughing and crying. Although epileptics certainly stand out by virtue of being unusually seizure-prone, susceptibility to seizures as such is a fundamental human experience, an existential factor in human life, and belongs to humankind just as much as seeing, conceptualizing, or sleeping and waking do.

It's difficult to tell just how long epilepsy has been around. We can only say that epilepsy, the tendency to seizures, or "falling sickness," as it has been called, is an age-old form of human suffering. I have my own ideas about the point of time in human history when epilepsy first came about, and perhaps I can give a few indications about it at the end of our three days' discussions. In any case, the "great suffering," as it was called in the Middle Ages, took hold of human beings long ago. Hippocrates, for example, already produced an extensive treatise on "falling sickness," as he called it then. Over and over again, down through the ages, epilepsy called forth anxiety and alarm in people witnessing seizures. For a long time it was considered an infectious illness, although there was as little truth in this as there is in the idea that it's hereditary. And it was only at the end of the nineteenth century that the brain came to be considered central to the illness, although we should let its exact role remain an open question for the time being. But in any case, the brain, with considerable justification, became the focus of research into epilepsy. There can be no doubt that we have to look to the central nervous system to find out what convulsive episodes hinge on. We'll try to work out just what the connection is during these two sessions.

So, as you see, humanity has been accompanied by seizures for thousands of years. In this, as in many areas of medicine, Hippocrates was the first to attempt to describe seizures precisely and to relate them to the principles of his medical philosophy. He also described them in connection with climatic influences, which is of great significance. Then this approach to the subject more or less disappeared until, with the dawn of modern scientific conceptions, the brain became the focus of investigation.

At the beginning of this century a real flood of findings began, which has increased right up to the present day. I consider it a significant achievement of modern medicine that we no longer debate what's "genuine" and what's "symptomatic" epilepsy. That the image of electric currents in the brain (electroencephalogram) of epileptics has been so thoroughly studied in recent times is also a significant chapter in modern human history, I believe. It's no coincidence that since the end of World War II, epilepsy has appeared in a totally new guise. And I mean that in an absolutely positive sense.

By now we have learned to classify seizures according to how they occur in the patients' rhythms of sleeping and waking and we also know that certain constitutional types belong to the so-called "sleep epileptics," others to the "waking epileptics"—that one person tends to have seizures at night, another in the morning upon awakening. Through detailed research, we've also learned to classify the forms of so-called "petit mal" that occur in childhood and to consider seizures in relationship to the seven-year periods of child development. If someone who knows only one or the other opens a book of anthroposophical spiritual science on the one hand and books of research on epilepsy on the other, they seem to have nothing to do with each other. But those familiar with both can be deeply grateful for the fact that in the case of grand or petit mal seizures, for instance, new connections can be found by taking into account indications of Rudolf Steiner's on the nature of the human being and of the developing child.

Let me repeat that epilepsy is not an isolated phenomenon, an obscure, terrifying, and peculiar illness. Every human being is a potential epileptic. We can only recognize epilepsy for what it is if we also understand human beings and their existential condition. Epilepsy cannot be understood without insight into the true nature of the human being. But the reverse may be equally true, that the human being cannot be understood independent of epilepsy. And so we must try to relate them to each other.

Jantz, one of the pioneers of modern epilepsy research, writes as follows: "Every human being will react to certain extreme conditions, such as severe electric shock, with an epileptic seizure. But we only speak of epilepsy as such when seizures occur for no apparent reason or are induced by circumstances (such as exhaustion, excessive intake of alcohol, or brain injury) which do not necessarily lead to seizures in every case, and when they occur repeatedly." Suppose someone receives a serious brain injury. One individual might react to this injury by having a seizure, which might not be the case at all with someone else. A brain tumor can cause an epileptic seizure or a series of seizures in one person, but not in another with a similar tumor in the same place. And you know that not everyone who indulges in alcohol to excess suffers a seizure as a consequence—unfortunately! To begin with, a seizure is nothing more than an unspecific reaction of the organism to an indisposition or overtaxation of the central nervous system. Only repeated seizures indicate that the person is threatened with the development of epilepsy as such if the seizures are not arrested somehow.

This transformation of our ideas about epilepsy is something quite new. As it turns out, none of what used to be said about epilepsy is true—that it's incurable or inherited, for instance, or that it's accompanied by certain typical changes in personality usually leading to insanity, or other things of that sort. What's the rule in one form of epilepsy may be the exception in another. We must realize that the popular picture of epilepsy was an artificial product of institutional psychiatric perspectives, and a necessarily negative one at that. Our way of looking at epilepsy has actually changed from a singular to a pluralistic one.

Let me read you something else. Vogel has this to say about what factors have to be considered today in the area of research on convulsive disorders (this is from 1961): "If you look at the field of epilepsy research today, you will see a picture of assiduous activity, diverse to the point of being confusing, that nevertheless tends to concentrate in certain focal points. The first focus is the ongoing observation and ever more detailed differentiation and statistical recording of different seizure patterns. A second has formed around recording and interpreting the electrophysiological phenomena accompanying seizures. A third is the rapid development of drug therapy for epileptics through experimental work with animals and the constant chemical synthesis of new anticonvulsants."[1]

It must be emphasized that the treatment of epilepsy has made extraordinary progress in the past thirty years, and especially in the past fifteen years, but it has also taken some steps backward at the same time. In any case, it has given us insights we wouldn't even have dared to imagine only a few years ago, insights which we'll still at least have to mention in the course of our conversations.

Vogel continues: "The clamor of objective findings seldom allows the quieter single voice of the patient's own self-perception to be heard. Psychotherapists, too, have beaten a modest retreat in the face of the victorious banners of anticonvulsant chemistry, as if the treatment of epilepsy had been reduced once and for all to the question of what kind of pills to take and how to take them."

Then he goes on, "In research totally given over to outer perceptible phenomena we need to remember the personal suffering involved. Illnesses and their processes are not only events in and of themselves that exist, take their course, and can be observed, but they happen to us, we suffer them; they acquire significance for us as part of our self-experience." Following this quotation, Vogel speaks at length about Dostoyevsky, and especially about the main character in *The Idiot*, Prince Myshkin. By means of the precisely introspective descriptions Dostoyevsky gives of epileptic seizures, Vogel attempts to characterize some existential traits of the epileptic. This side of the picture should not be forgotten. Psychological studies of the subconscious such as those conducted by Brautigam several years ago reveal (and I believe it is justified to speak like this) that the epileptic has a day and a night side. Of course, so does every other human being. But in the epileptic, the day side is brighter and the shadow side is darker. In the field of tension in which all human beings find themselves, the epileptic's existence is much more highly charged. The fear, doubt, fright, anxiety, despair, melancholy, and mania that such a person has to go through are, although human, excessive in every way, which is something we must take into account.

And after all his studies, a man like Vogel whom I just quoted cannot help but conclude by pointing out that "at the end of his short life, Raphael painted a glorious picture in which two successive stories from the Gospel are united and related to each other. The lower half of the painting depicts the presentation of the epileptic boy to the disciples. Above it, as if in a transcendent space, is the Transfiguration of Jesus, from which the painting has received its title." He notes that the bottom half of the painting has been reproduced in a famous textbook by Lennox, the leading American researcher in the field of epilepsy, and then concludes, "Now, it seems to me that it's not doing an injustice to Lennox and his work if we let this fragment of the painting he chose as the guiding image for his work remind us from time to time of the larger, complete picture, and let our scientific inquiries stand under that sign." Vogel can permit himself this shattering statement only because we touch on the very core of human existence when we investigate epilepsy, and unless we really go as far as that core, any attempt we make to say something real and concrete about epilepsy will be in vain. Let's take this as our starting point.

What is it that's so horrifying to someone who has to witness a seizure? Perhaps it can be said in a single word. People who aren't accustomed to these episodes are horrified by the *dehumanization* taking place before their very eyes. I'll give a few examples. An infant of seven or eight months is sitting up, alert and cheerful. All of a sudden his gaze becomes fixed, his head falls forward, his hands and arms move apart. This is repeated several times in quick succession and then everything is fine again. A child like this can have these so-called "nodding" or "bowing" seizures 30, 40, 60, 80 times a day and may be seriously handicapped in his intellectual development unless they can be arrested. Another example: A girl, let's say—I'm taking examples I remember—eight or nine years old is sitting in school working on an assignment, when suddenly she goes red in the face, her head falls back, her eyes roll upward, and she trembles as she tries to go on writing. You can tell that she's not fully "there." After two or three seconds, her consciousness clears and she goes on writing as if nothing had happened. An 11- or 12-year old boy sits at the breakfast table. Suddenly, without warning, one arm begins to twitch. He grasps a plate and throws it on the floor, then comes to his senses and turns red because he suddenly notices that something has happened to him and that he was totally unaware of it. This often happens daily, mostly in the morning. In some cases it occurs only at greater intervals.

I won't mention the names of these conditions yet; I'm only describing them. Some other examples: Sometimes you'll find a child who is eight, five, or sometimes even younger who suddenly begins to make faces, to do something strange with her mouth—and just as suddenly it's over. You get the impression that she was semiconscious. In most instances, she doesn't even fall over. She may even withdraw into a corner of the room, because this kind of episode or seizure, or whatever we want to call it, may last up to ten minutes. Or we can be talking with an adult, having an intense conversation, when suddenly he says, "It's coming" and goes and lies down on the couch. The left side of his face begins to twitch, and then his left hand and arm; it spreads from his face into his shoulder. Finally it becomes a generalized convulsion of the whole left side of his body, but his eyes are open and it's quite possible for him to remain conscious through the whole thing.

Next we must go on to look at the "big seizures" or grand mal. This is what is always associated with the word "epilepsy," although it's actually only one sector out of the whole circle of convulsive seizures of different degrees, with or without loss of consciousness. A grand mal can begin in many different ways, quite individually. People who are aware of their condition and able to maintain consciousness in the early stages of a seizure will tell you individually very different things that appear at the beginning of such an episode—perhaps a particular odor or impression of color. Little children may run and seek the protection of their mother, saying, "It hurts here." An older child may say, "I feel warmth rising up, and then I get dizzy." Another person may tell you, "As a child I was once very badly frightened. Whenever the memory of that event rises up in me and overcomes me, I know a seizure's coming." That's how much the so-called "auras" may differ from person to person. An initial cry or scream often though not always comes next, and then the person collapses. At first there's a tonic stiffening of the muscles, which then gives way to clonic twitching or jerking. Breathing and circulation are disturbed, and body temperature may rise. Then the convulsions cease and a kind of stupor spreads over the person. The stupor passes over into a shorter or longer period of sleep, and the whole thing is over. (For the moment I won't speak about after-effects of seizures.)

I've described the kinds of phenomena which can appear, but you mustn't believe that this sufficiently characterizes their scope and diversity. You could almost say that just as each human being dies the death that belongs to him or her, so too each person has his or her own individual seizure pattern that changes in the course of the years from childhood through adolescence to old age, but is still not to be confused with anyone else's.

At this point we may wonder whether there's any deeper way of characterizing the seizures we've just described. I believe there is. I believe we can say that, on the one hand, we are faced primarily with a loss of consciousness in both petit mal and grand mal. In general, loss of consciousness is part of the total picture of a seizure episode, although it need not be a total loss of consciousness. The other determining factor in a seizure is the cramp or convulsion. It can be a generalized convulsion or specific to one, two, or three limbs, the face, or any other part of the body. Once we've singled out these two factors, we can already define things more clearly. Loss of consciousness, on the one hand, means that the world, a human being's environment, disappears as far as he or she is concerned. Awareness of one's surroundings is lost. This is one sign of what we called dehumanization. The other is the convulsive episode, which we may describe by saying that without his or her knowledge or participation, a person's body is taken hold of by an event over which that person has no control.

This means that the human being is attacked from two sides, on the sensory side where waking consciousness is maintained, and at the same time on the motor side, where the body and its movements are controlled. Once we've recognized these two things, loss of consciousness through the senses being extinguished and loss of one's own physical nature through the motor system being thrown into convulsions, the convulsive seizure becomes transparent. What is it that's actually happening? To answer this, we need to refer back to a chapter in our earlier anthroposophical studies of the human being. Since we've already dealt with this in our courses together, I'll only mention it briefly. We spoke again and again about the threefold human being, of the upper pole of the nerves and senses, of the rhythmic person and of the metabolic-limb person. We know that we are awake in the first area, for our existence in concepts, thoughts and memories, mediated by our senses, gives us waking consciousness. We know that we're only dreaming in our emotions, and that this dream-consciousness only enters our waking consciousness when feelings become concepts. If we're so involved in sympathy or antipathy toward some being or thing that the experience becomes conscious, then feelings become concepts and dreams become consciousness. And everything that has to do with the metabolic-limb or motor system remains in a state of sleep even when we're awake. I know that I want to pick up this piece of chalk, but I haven't the foggiest idea how my fingers actually get over there—guided or not guided by my eyes, as the case may be—and do it. Again, I know that I have picked it up. I know what I intend to do, but I'm asleep in these legs moving toward the chalkboard. You are asleep in your legs as you sit. We are all asleep in every act of will we perform. That's simply a fact of human existence. So we have consciousness on the one hand (by which I mean day-consciousness), and then the other side which we can call the side of the will, of motor activity, and of sleep.

Now let's ask ourselves what happens when a person, who could be any one of us, has a seizure. Let's assume it's a grand mal, to make things easier. What happens is that the three stages of consciousness are displaced upwards. Waking is displaced outside the head; dreaming takes hold of the sensory-nervous pole; sleep, will, and motor activity invade the rhythmic system. This first step in considering seizures is a kind of framework we'll use later on to make our observations more specific. You can see right away what has to happen for a seizure to come about. Dreaming takes hold of the head, and what happens? The aura, with its floods of color, trickles of tastes and smells, uncontrollable images, or peculiar dream-figures, takes hold of conceptual activity. We can say that what usually takes place within the confines of the middle organization moves up a step and penetrates the sensory-nervous sphere. Motor activity also breaks through into the middle organization, that is, the limbs begin to twitch in a way that normally belongs only to the beating heart. The rhythm of the heart, and sometimes that of the breath as well, spreads out over the whole muscular system. The lower part of the person assumes the place of the middle, the upper part is penetrated by the middle system, and waking consciousness is pushed out altogether, that is, the head no longer exerts any influence. We could speak at length about how the head "gets lost"—the head that otherwise governs (I didn't say "directs" or "causes") every movement of the limbs, the head from which tranquility streams so that excessive movement is kept in check. The head, along with our waking awareness of the sensory world, is lost. The middle organization and feeling move upward, and since the middle has become empty, it is invaded by the otherwise sleeping will, which takes over all motor activity. This is a first archetypal image of what happens in a seizure.

If you study the phenomena of different types of seizures—take a case of Jacksonian epilepsy, for instance—you'll notice that these seizures invariably begin on the periphery, perhaps in the fingers, moving upwards into the arms and shoulders. Or a seizure may begin in one cheek or on the forehead, but it invariably begins on the periphery and then moves toward the center. The seizure attacks the person from outside. The convulsions force their way from the periphery toward the center, that is, the person is literally "attacked" by the seizure. Tomorrow and the next day we will talk about what it is that "attacks" or "seizes" the person from outside. But you can already imagine the situation of a person being overcome by a seizure. Something attacks from outside, displacing the sleeping will-person into the middle organization and the middle organization into the head, and world and body are both lost as far as the person, the individual, the individuality is concerned.

And now let's attempt to approach this event from another angle. In January 1924, when Rudolf Steiner took up his teaching activity anew, he characterized the modern human being by pointing to two very particular questions that are (if we may put it like that) rumbling around in the depths of human soul-existence. These are questions that don't often rise up into our daytime consciousness, but that are nevertheless alive in every human being whether he or she knows it or not. One question is, "Where does my human form actually come from, this *Gestalt* that is not to be found in the same form anywhere else in the world?" When, after our death, the world takes hold of this form and the forces of the world intrude upon it, only one thing is possible—the destruction of this form. And on the other hand, a second question is alive in every human being: "Nature surrounds me, but this nature is inaccessible to me in its essential being, for what I perceive of the beings and forms of nature is actually only semblance." Rudolf Steiner formulated it as follows: "If we human beings intrude into the world out there, it will destroy us. It will not tolerate the presence of our own essential being within it. Nor is it possible for the external world to enter human souls.

Our thoughts are mere images, external to the essence and being of things. Stones' being, being of plants, animals, stars, clouds, can never enter the human soul. The world surrounding us human beings cannot reach our soul, but remains outside." This can be expressed aphoristically: "Nature exists, but we human beings can only approach it by letting ourselves be destroyed by it. The human soul exists, but nature can only reach this human soul by becoming an illusion."[2] If you really take this in, you'll soon see that it contains the two central questions of our human existence in seed form: "Nature exists, but we can only approach it by letting ourselves be destroyed by it. The human soul exists, but nature can only reach this human soul by becoming an illusion."

I only need to write the words "semblance" and "destruction" on the board, and anyone who has dealt with epileptics and is aware of their make-up, or has seriously tried to understand his or her own make-up, will know that human beings in general and epileptics in particular stand between these two poles of semblance and destruction, which we must confront daily, continually, and unflinchingly. This is the characteristic signature of epilepsy, a signature we may in good conscience call "susceptibility to seizures."

The world we take in through our senses is a semblance, and we must continually live as if we took it for real. We have to, because we couldn't exist otherwise. We have to live in the world of appearances "as if" it were real. (I use the phrase "as if" with caution because it can be attributed to an old and untrue philosophical system.) That is our human condition. On the other hand, we live in the depths of the destruction with which nature is constantly threatening us. This destruction is present in all processes of digestion taking place in us and in every motor activity we perform from morning till night, and we must constantly push it aside and forget it. Human beings exist within this duality or tension or tremendous polarity between the semblance of reality and the oblivion and destruction brought on by forces threatening us from below. If I may use an image to make myself understood better, I would say that we maintain ourselves in the world of semblance with the shield of our consciousness; we maintain ourselves against the destructive forces assailing us with the spear of our egohood, our individuality. If either the shield or the sword breaks, then destruction forces its way upward, the illusory image cracks, and, unexpectedly and unbearably, Being breaks through the appearances.

This is what Dostoyevsky describes when he has Prince Myshkin say of his initial aura and seizure, "It is something not of the earth, by which I don't mean that it's something heavenly, but only that a person in an earthly body cannot withstand it, but must either change physically, or die. This is a clear and incontestable feeling. If it were to last longer than five seconds, the soul would be unable to bear it and would have to succumb. A total physical transformation is required in order to withstand it for even ten seconds." You see, this is what's really at stake behind the question of epilepsy. If a person's shield of consciousness cracks, something unendurable suddenly streams in, and in order to bear it the body must be transformed, as Prince Myshkin puts it. People often even assume a characteristic stance at a particular point in a seizure. Or, if the spear doesn't work, the powers of destruction rise up from below, forcing the soul upwards, and the whole structure of consciousness is changed. And just because, as we'll discuss tomorrow, a human being maintains uprightness between gravity and light, if the light is extinguished, the person collapses and a seizure occurs. That's what happens to all those people who are sent into the hell of a seizure—that's how they describe it—because of insulin shock or electric shock. I'm not saying anything to confirm or refute this; I'm only describing what people say who have had to go through experiences withheld from the rest of us only by virtue of the fact that we manage to maintain ourselves in our threefoldness between semblance and destruction.

2. Different Types of Convulsive Disorders

We've already noted that a convulsive "seizure" or "attack" is just that—the words describe it very aptly and accurately. The whole motor system is "attacked" or "seized" by something other than the human being in question, or, if you will, something different from the conscious human being who's otherwise in possession of this motor system. When a seizure occurs, the person's conscious motivation is hardly able to resist it—in fact, it's usually wiped out by the seizure. Those of you who remember how we talked about spastic and athetotic types of paralysis may comment that these are also conditions in which the motor system is attacked in such a way that the person, be it a child or a teenager or an adult, cannot completely master his or her motor activity. Hemiplegia, for instance, can make free and deliberate movement of one arm and one leg impossible. In athetotic paralysis, a different and often conflicting impulse enters the moment the motivation to do something comes about, making it impossible for the person to accomplish what he or she actually wanted to do. Thus we can say that we're dealing with a quasi-convulsive attack on the motor system in athetoid spasticity. Phenomenologically, it's similar to what comes to light suddenly and acutely in a true seizure, at least in one side of it. We've related the other side to a change in, or loss of, consciousness. These two things—loss of consciousness on the one hand, and the effect on the motor system on the other, are the determining factors in a seizure episode.

Different stages in this change of consciousness are possible. A waking state of consciousness may be maintained during the seizure, or, as in a psychomotor seizure, a kind of groggy semi-conscious state may set in. This semi-consciousness can lead over into dreaming, the dreaming to unconsciousness, unconsciousness to deep sleep. As with the convulsions, it is not simply an either/or question with regard to consciousness during a seizure; different degrees of consciousness are possible. I've already tried to show how the stages of consciousness are displaced during a grand mal, so that sleeping consciousness takes over the dreaming middle organization, the dreaming middle organization takes hold of the head's waking consciousness, and the head's waking consciousness disappears altogether. This led us to observe our own make-up in relationship to epileptic seizures. In this process we came to a clear interpretation of our existence and realized that inasmuch as our senses reveal the world to us, this world is actually only a kind of semblance.

Do I really have to explain all this? Aren't we all aware of it? When the philosophers of the last century were struggling with problems of epistemology, their question was always the same: "How do I recognize reality in what is revealed to me through my eyes and ears, through touch and all my other senses? How do I recognize it in these reflections in my soul?" We've learned from Rudolf Steiner that perception of reality is possible, but only to be attained and experienced by means of extreme effort. In itself, everything we meet, and especially everything we perceive with our eyes, is a world of semblances. All of us are locked into this world of appearances, and this is particularly true of the epileptic. Doesn't the world vanish and take flight every night when we go to sleep, and sink into a darkness in which we often completely forget even our dream experiences?

But in the very moment of waking in the morning or in moments of waking during the night, the illusory world of sense perceptions immediately appears to us so that we become conscious.

Years ago, the psychiatrist Strumpel already experimented with making his patients fall asleep by shutting off sense-impressions. He plugged their ears and bandaged their eyes, and in most cases did succeed in getting them to fall asleep. This makes it immediately apparent that the world of semblance to which our consciousness clings is a sensory world. This is one of two things that fall apart when a seizure begins. The other is the motor system. I've already mentioned that movement begins the moment we wake up and that as long as we're conscious, it only ceases in very particular moments—during meditation or elevated prayer, for instance, or perhaps when we're totally given up to some strong sense impression. Otherwise, though, our motor system is constantly in motion, regardless of whether we're sitting or standing, lying or walking, speaking or working. We reveal ourselves with our ego, our individuality, to others and to the world through our motor system, but we cannot achieve cognition through it. I reminded you of two sayings of Rudolf Steiner's that characterize the dual situation of the human being very clearly. He says, "The human soul exists, but nature can only approach it by becoming an illusory image. Nature exists, but human beings can only reach it if they allow themselves to be destroyed by it." Thus each human being stands between semblance and destruction. The seizure-prone person is trapped between consciousness above and motor activity down below, and since we've learned that all human beings are capable of seizures, this also applies to every one of us. Now let's go one step further and look at the different types of convulsive disorders that have been documented in the last few decades. It's quite extraordinary to look a bit more closely at the phenomena of different forms of epilepsy. The different movement patterns appearing at different stages of life are not arbitrary, but are age-specific, that is, the seizure patterns of infants are different from those of school children and those of adolescents.[1] In recognizing these different seizure patterns, it is essential (and astonishing) to note that one pattern can evolve into another, but only at the appropriate age. For example, the movement pattern of infantile seizures can develop into the typical pattern of a school-age child, but it is totally impossible for a pattern typical of the school-child or adolescent to revert to one belonging to a younger child. Regression of patterns does not occur. Please keep in mind that these symptoms are biologically determined and are intimately related to the developmental stage of the child. Now all we need to do is solve the riddle a pattern like this presents so that we can perceive what it's trying to tell us.

While these movement patterns are age-specific, varying according to different developmental stages, there are other seizure patterns belonging to the grand mal type which are not age-specific. They may also appear in infancy, but in this case it's not the movement patterns of the seizures that are characteristic, but the rhythmic intervals at which they occur. They are bound, not to a certain time of day, to midnight, noon, or 8 o'clock in the morning or evening, but to a person's individual rhythm of sleeping and waking. One person falls asleep at midnight, while another who works the night shift may only get to sleep at six in the morning. It isn't the time of day that matters, but rather the individual timing of the person who wakes up and falls asleep. Once again we're confronted with something biologically determined, in this case, something bound to the rhythm of changes in consciousness through waking and sleeping.

When we look at it like this, we can immediately grasp the two different aspects of a seizure, the sensory or consciousness aspect and the motor aspect. We begin to understand that the pattern presented by the motor pole is age-specific, whereas consciousness is related to the time when a seizure occurs, to the day/night or, better, the sleep/waking rhythm of the person in question. Once again, we have before us the two main pillars of a seizure—on the one hand, loss of consciousness and overcoming illusion; and on the other, destruction with regard to motor control.

And now I must go back to something we worked on before, something we must always return to in order to understand child development. I described for you how a newborn child sets out on a dual path of what we call incarnation. On the one hand, we have incarnation into our physical nature. We take hold of our physical existence stage after stage and step by step throughout childhood and adolescence. On the other hand, we also begin to recognize the world, a process we called "discrimination." We begin to differentiate among the beings and objects of the world, which the infant still experiences vividly as flowing together in a unity. We reach out into the world through our senses; we reach down into our body by means of our motor activity. These are the guiding images that make our body into the tool of our Self and the world into the object of our existence.

Once we've acquired the right archetypal images, we meet them everywhere, again and again. One, as we know by now, is world/semblance/senses—the transformation of consciousness in the day-and-night rhythm of a seizure. On the other hand, we also meet our own body, motor activity, and incarnation—the pole of destruction which we must constantly resist.

Age-specific patterns apply to the motor aspect of seizures. I've already tried to present these briefly; now let's look at them more closely. Primarily because of work done by Americans, but also through the Heidelberg School, we've learned more and more about the phenomena of the so-called "petit mal triad"—three different groups of motoric seizure patterns. The first group consists of different types of spasms with onset in infancy. In this connection, the most important thing to note about infantile spasms is that the child's head is actively involved in the motor disturbance provoked by the seizure. These spasms start with the head and then spread out to include the arms and chest, or even the entire body. "Nodding" and "bowing" spasms are more or less restricted to the head and upper body, but there's another type that starts at the head and shoots through the child's whole body like a bolt of lightning. With the help of fairly recently developed forms of medical treatment, or sometimes even without, these convulsions can often disappear as the child grows and develops. But the intellectual development of children like this is frequently impaired or delayed.

In the next stage of development, in pre-school and school-age children, the so-called "absences" appear. They also take many different forms, but in spite of the variety, it is still possible to recognize them as such. Just as it's possible to tell whether an animal is a dog or a cat in spite of the many different breeds of dogs and cats, it's also possible to tell that an absence is an absence.

These absences are light seizures which are often overlooked in the early stages or mistaken for some kind of naughty behavior. A little boy may be walking with his parents, chattering away, when suddenly he stops, stares, takes a couple of steps in a different direction, and then wakes up and goes on talking as if he'd never stopped. Or you might see a girl sitting in school, paying attention to what the teacher is saying, when suddenly her chin drops, her eyelids close, and her head falls backward. After a few seconds, she's conscious again. These absences can take any possible form of head-turning, blinking, eye-rolling, and so on. But the basic form is always the same—a sudden loss of consciousness, especially of the kind of day-consciousness connected with light and looking and seeing, with no involvement of the motor system. That's the second type of petit mal.

The third group of seizures are called myoclonic seizures or impulsive petit mals. Imagine a teenager washing the dishes for his or her mother. She suddenly notices how the child begins to tremble. Then a dish gets tossed into the air and breaks. Or, while the child is getting dressed, one or the other limb begins to twitch. These episodes often happen in the morning. Sometimes they happen in very quick succession, like a whole volley of shots being fired.

If we chart the age of onset of these three groups of seizures, we find that infantile spasms begin most frequently during the first three years of life, peaking around age one. Absences peak between the seventh and eighth years and appear primarily during the second seven-year period. Impulsive petit mals encompass primarily the third seven-year period, peaking at around the fifteenth year of life.[2] This is really noteworthy. What does it tell us? Nothing other than what Rudolf Steiner said again and again, that children go through three distinct seven-year periods of development, the first lasting until the change of teeth, the second until puberty, and the third until around age twenty when full maturity is reached. Now we can ask what it all means. What is the significance of the age-related pattern of the petit mal triad?

Allow me to make use of an image. If you see a baby suffering from these spasmodic movements, you get the impression that a storm is gathering overhead in distant rumblings and flashes of heat-lightning. If you remember what heat-lightning is like and apply this image, you'll see how it fits this kind of seizure episode. And if you see absences in a school child, you get the impression that a cloud has passed over and cut off the light of consciousness. If you observe impulsive petit mals next, it's as if the lightning really begins to strike. Staying with this image, the storm announces its coming during the first seven-year period; the clouds gather during the second; the lightning begins during the third, and then the storm breaks when the grand mals begin. I know this is no scientific explanation—I didn't intend to give one, but only to characterize this three-step build-up in a way you won't forget.

What do we find on closer examination of all this? In the case of the infantile spasms, loss of consciousness and a quick, tremor-like convulsion still go together. Later on, they separate—an absence is simply a loss of consciousness, and impulsive petit mals are a motor disturbance. In the course of development, the original combination of the two turns into a simple loss of consciousness first and, later, into a motor disturbance only. In the end, both come together again in the grand mal. This is the way seizures develop, and there's no going back. These are the changing forms seizures assume from the first to the second to the third seven-year period.

The second period differs from the first in that what Zeller characterized as the child's first transformation of physique takes place between them, during the sixth or seventh year.[3] He described in detail how the child's whole body becomes elongated during the second dentition. If we ask what's happening just then, we can arrive at a clear answer if we go by what Rudolf Steiner told us about this event—that until the fifth or sixth year, children are basically determined by their heads, and that a small child's head extends down into the lower body as well. When this stage is over, the body begins to elongate, and the head becomes something separate that can begin to think. Once this has happened, the child can learn and remember and repeat what's been learned.

An infant, because it's all head and its feet don't quite reach down to the earth yet, gets these sudden spasms like flashes of heat-lightning. In the second seven-year period, the world begins to enter the child's consciousness, and the now separate head can hide or withdraw from this world, so absences set in. Please don't try to psychoanalyze this—I simply mean it as it appears phenomenologically. It's only during the third seven-year period that human beings really enter into their limbs. If they don't take hold of them completely, those impulsive petit mals we described as flashes of lightning come about, just as absences come about when someone can't make his or her head separate completely. That's the statement we can make about petit mal seizures.

Those who know Rudolf Steiner's work well will be able to relate all this to the "three births" he spoke about—the birth of the physical body, the birth of the life-body around age seven, and later the birth of the soul in the fourteenth year. The results of research on epilepsy reveal the facts of spiritual science. That researchers today have so little possibility of asking *why* is due to a lack of insight on their part—insight they could have if they only wanted to.

Now that we've described the different age-specific

patterns of motor involvement, the next step has to do with the rhythm of sleeping and waking. Results are available from investigations begun over fifteen years ago and still going on. We've learned from them to distinguish three forms of grand mal epilepsy. One is so-called waking epilepsy, the second is sleep epilepsy, and the third is diffuse epilepsy.

Surveys taken in recent years among a large group of general practitioners in Wales show that about 10% of all people are seizure-prone—that is, they've had one or the other seizure at some point without further consequences. It remains a family secret, so to speak. Approximately four or five percent have a seizure or some kind of seizure-like condition every so often at very great intervals, and at the top of this broad-based pyramid you get the very narrow tip of those with chronic seizures—.4 to .5% of the population. We were talking about these four or five people out of a thousand when we mentioned the three forms of grand mal epilepsy.

Waking and sleep epilepsy are rhythm-related, but diffuse epilepsy is not, that is, the seizures of someone suffering from diffuse epilepsy can happen at any time of day or night. Waking epileptics can have seizures at two specific times of day. When they wake up in the morning, they wake up with difficulty. They belong to the kind of person (and I think we can also include many of ourselves at times) who actually doesn't want to go to bed at night, but prefers to spend time with friends, drinking and talking and discussing and debating. Once the others have left, they're suddenly full of ideas and still want to write something down, or absolutely have to prepare something for the next day. When they lie down, the thoughts keep on turning around in their heads, and they think, "I want to go to sleep, but I don't *really* want to sleep." When they finally do fall asleep, they wake up again in between, and only fall into deep sleep toward morning. If they have to wake up at that point, they actually can't, and that's when their seizures strike. This is typical of waking epileptics. They recover quickly, because the world distracts them. Waking epileptics are devoted to the outer world. They are active people, trying out and doing this, that and the other thing to the point of excess. Once the day is over, they think to themselves, "Now I can finally do something for myself." They come home and sit down, and then another seizure occurs. This is called "free-time epilepsy." So waking epileptics tend to have seizures in connection with the process of waking up in the morning, in some instances even before they wake up, and then again in the evening once the intensity of the working day has subsided.

If you read *The Idiot* by Dostoyevsky, as I hope many of you will do, after these lectures, you'll find a typical waking epileptic in the character of Prince Myshkin—a large, tall, thin, asthenic type with long slender hands, always a bit ecstatic, reaching out beyond himself, a true saint in some respects because there's so much of the child in him, but a dark character in others, a man who's only able to escape an attempt on his life by means of a seizure. These are the two sides of the waking epileptic. He is an extremist in the excessive brightness of ecstasy and in the darkness of the night side of his existence.

Typical sleep epileptics are quite different. They're the kind who sleep most deeply immediately after going to sleep and gradually wake up toward morning. Their seizures can occur at any point during the process of falling asleep, but they can also happen somewhat differently. Many of you will have experienced something similar without going as far as a seizure. Before they fall asleep for good, they fall asleep and wake up again, but wake up into a seizure. Imagine yourself falling asleep and waking up again suddenly, with a jerk, like falling down a mountain. In this instance, sleep epileptics wouldn't wake up, but would fall into their sleep epilepsy, which is why I said they wake up in a seizure. (Of course they don't become conscious when they wake up like that.) They are totally different people from waking epileptics. Sleep epileptics are sufficient unto themselves, but more often in a narrow than in a nice way. They are pedantic, slow, and clingy, emphasize the inessential and don't see the essential.

Now what's actually going on in these two extremes? Let's imagine these two figures, the pedant and the somewhat ecstatic Prince Myshkin. (I'm exaggerating, of course, to make myself understood and to present the archetypal phenomenon clearly.) One of them can't sleep at night and the other lies down and has a seizure immediately. You may wonder what it is in sleep epileptics that makes them ruminate on words and sentences over and over again, unable to let go. They are people who cling convulsively, as it were, to day-consciousness, but sleep gets the better of them, and they plunge into the depths of destruction. The others, the waking epileptics, are the ones who don't want to enter the day, who shrink back from the world of semblances. Basically, they'd prefer not to wake up at all, because semblance is not sufficient for them. One extreme hangs on tight, while the other wants to get beyond the appearances into a still brighter light.

Once we've realized that waking epileptics are ecstatic because they yearn for a transcendent existence, we can recognize the relationship between the three different adult types of epileptics that have been discovered in recent years. You'll recall that within the petit mal triad, the seizure pattern of the first seven years can only develop into the pattern typical of the school-child and then into that typical of adolescence. The reverse is not possible. Something similar is also the case here. You see, waking epilepsy can only develop into sleep epilepsy. It can then go on to become diffuse epilepsy, just as sleep epilepsy can also develop into diffuse epilepsy. This progression is possible, but the reverse is not. It's possible to sink down from waking epilepsy into sleep epilepsy and then into diffuse epilepsy, because this is a degenerative process. (I don't mean that in the moral sense.) It's possible to sink down from striving for light into being bound by the sensory world, and from there into the relative dullness and debility of diffuse epilepsy.

What do waking epileptics aspire to? They want to break through the mirror of sensory appearances, to reach out beyond the day-consciousness to which sleep epileptics cling because they are afraid to plunge into the depths of sleep. Now that we've made all these observations, we must still add what Rudolf Steiner told us in so many different ways about waking and sleeping or we won't be able to take the next step toward understanding the phenomena we've described.

What happens when we fall asleep? As far as our higher existence, our soul and spirit-being, is concerned, we go out, we expand, we breathe out into the world of macrocosmic existence by flowing out through our limbs. We flow out into the expanses of the world where our soul breathes out, then returns toward morning in an act of inhalation, concentration, or contraction out of the periphery toward the head.

It's characteristic of waking epileptics that they don't want to become concentrated, but would rather remain out there, bringing things to consciousness that would otherwise remain unconscious. It's the fate of sleep epileptics to be unable to let go enough to enter the expanses of existence by falling asleep, and then to fall after all and be destroyed. You see, this isn't far removed from what's taking place in each one of us all the time. Once again, we see the two poles of motor activity/ destruction and consciousness/waking. By means of this formulation, we begin to be able to shed some light on the various phenomena of epileptic existence and to comprehend them. Epileptics themselves, however, are not able to describe what they experience.

But by now you should be able to see what's needed by way of treatment. You can see in principle exactly what we need to do for one extreme and the other. We must relieve the sleep epileptics' fear of the expanses and of letting go. We must loosen them up. This can be done through music—that's a means of bringing a bit of healing to sleep epileptics. Waking epileptics must push through to the supersensible by means of image and color. This can in no way replace the necessary medication, of course, but it can complement it significantly.

3. Epilepsy and Hysteria

As long as we don't have the courage to take the distilled and essential concepts of spiritual science into consideration, as long as we don't have the courage to really ask what happens when a human being sleeps, what happens to us when we wake up, when through the waking process the body lying in bed becomes the tool of our Self once again, we're not asking the right questions. We still have the impression that some substance or tissue in the brain is the sole basis of what we call consciousness, which comes about when we wake up and disappears when we go to sleep. We need to stop reacting from the point of view of psychology, automatically rejecting the concept of consciousness because we can't determine anything about it from outside and denying it the right to exist because inner observation is subjective, i.e., unscientific. As long as we don't try to overcome these ideas in ourselves as individuals, we won't achieve any degree of insight, no matter how compelling the phenomena confronting us may be.

When I attempt to speak about epilepsy, it's not simply a question of describing being epileptic or hysteric. The main thing is to recognize the anthropological reality behind these conditions in such a way that we start to confront and understand ourselves as individuals and as human beings. We tried to describe convulsive seizures by separating them into two component parts—the convulsion or cramp on the one hand, and everything having to do with a loss of or change in consciousness on the other. We also described the different forms of seizures typical of childhood and adolescence. And now that we're approaching the end of our deliberations, it seems natural and right that we should ask ourselves the following question. "Do all the different forms of seizures within the broad spectrum of seizure-susceptibility have anything in common? Do they have a common background that might disclose itself to us?"

Although the question may sound strange at first, we really do need to ask what a convulsion is, what its significance and purpose may be. We noticed that seizures in childhood and adolescence are different from the grand mals appearing in adulthood. What do babies and school children and adolescents in the petit mal triad and adults in waking and sleep epilepsy have in common? Or are they essentially different phenomena? That's really the question.

I want to go through the different forms of seizures again, step by step, with different questions in mind than yesterday and the day before. First of all, the petit mal triad. A spasm in a baby, an infant. We can induce a seizure like this by allowing too strong a light to shine on the child, or by making a loud noise, or by calling the child's name from behind. When we do that, the child can go into one of the types of infantile spasms. If we take the next step to classic absence seizures, you'll frequently notice that these children will often have an absence if they stop and hesitate over a task, if they get into a situation they can't master immediately, or if they're suddenly asked something like, "Tell me right away—how much is 5673 minus 3229?" Things like that will probably induce an absence. And if you ask a twelve-, fourteen-, or sixteen-year old boy who's prone to impulsive petit mals to do something that's difficult for him, he'll often fall into those convulsive movements (especially if it's in the morning). When we ask ourselves what the common basis for all this is, it's in a sense justified to say that in all the cases I described, the people in question are unable to respond to being called upon, to a request to be alert and make an effort. Not enough presence of mind or "presence of spirit" is available for them to live up to the demand or challenge. Epileptics respond to attempts to wake them up with a retreat—the infant with a spasm, the school child with an absence, the teenager with a convulsion. Basically, increased wakefulness is called for and increased attentiveness needed, but this wakefulness and attentiveness are not achieved. The pendulum swings the other way, resulting in a retreat of some sort. Once we can begin to conceive of it like this, then it seems to me that we've gotten quite a bit closer to answering the question of what underlies seizures in general.

Let's go on and look at the grand mal. We spoke about waking epileptics and sleep epileptics and tried to describe sleep epileptics as the ones who try to maintain consciousness at all costs, but don't succeed, and then have seizures in the process of falling asleep, just as waking epileptics have seizures when they're waking up from deep sleep and trying to get up.

Before we go on, let me add something of greatest importance. People's morning and evening rituals are of extraordinary significance. We all have them, and it's basically pretty difficult for many of us (especially as we get older, but also for younger people) to travel from place to place because it takes a day or two for us to adjust these rituals to our altered circumstances. It's one of the most interesting observations you can make about children (you don't often get the chance with adults) to see how they get dressed or undressed, for instance, whether a boy puts his shirt or his pants on first, or slips into his socks and shoes before pulling on his pants and throws his shirt over his head last, or whether he brushes his teeth first, then combs his hair, and washes his face last, or the other way around. Believe me, you can achieve quite a bit in the way of rehabilitation if you begin to change an epileptic's or also a hysteric's rituals conscientiously, gently, and step by step. There's practically nothing as deeply inscribed in habit as these morning and evening rituals, which are often seizure-substitutes. I mean that in all seriousness.

Observe how children dress themselves dreamily in the morning and just barely get damp when they wash. Basically, they only really come to and wake up once they've had something to drink or a bite to eat. If you really observe that, you begin to smell, taste, and perceive how the human being who's out there in the world during sleep once again begins to take hold of this physical organism with its eyes, nose, ears, mouth, head, and chest step by step. Vegetative functions can be proceeding perfectly normally, but everything that has to do with becoming conscious or with motor activity is apt to be clumsy in the morning, especially when it isn't possible to perform our usual rituals. The bad moods we ourselves get into in such cases are the same bad moods from which the epileptic suffers so deeply and with which he makes his surroundings suffer. I know many people who can be quite charming after eleven o'clock in the morning. Before that, they're insufferable, and well aware of that fact. How difficult children can be in the morning, how wild they can get in the evening! That's because in the evening they're already on the way out and can't hold themselves together anymore, and in the morning, they're still in a semi-conscious state when they're supposed to be awake already.

I'm telling you this so that you'll finally get the idea that these things are at least as important as an electroencephalogram. I have nothing against EEGs; on the contrary. But I am very much opposed to the fact that they're the only thing that counts as valid, and that every effort to observe the *human* phenomena of waking and sleeping is rejected as being subjective and therefore irrelevant. If we go on like this, we're going to lose all our humanity, not just in research, but in the rest of our life as well.

Let's get back to the questions we were asking earlier. What happens in the case of waking epileptics? We said yesterday that they come into their bodies; they try to wake up, but basically they don't want the world of appearances. The glass between them and reality breaks, and they do wake up, but into a seizure. That's saying quite a lot. Sleep epileptics cling to the sensory world, not wanting to lose themselves in sleep or to give up their identity to the expanses of night and darkness. They want to hang on to the world of semblances, but falling asleep forces them to let go. They are called back and wake up, but also in a seizure.

As soon as we've recognized this, we can tell what all seizures have in common; namely, that they're all nothing more than unsuccessful attempts to wake up. These people wake up in a seizure; their attempt at waking up fails. In every seizure, waking up is wanted and attempted, but the attempt fails, and in the moment of failure a seizure sets in. If whenever you see a grand mal or a petit mal, you tell yourself that an attempt at waking has failed, that this person is inside his or her bodily organization, but woke up wrong, then you've come quite a bit closer to solving the riddle of the epileptic condition.

This is the terrible frustration epileptics suffer under and that causes all their bad moods. Their whole situation in life is due to a continuous abortive attempt to wake up. It's always the same, whether it leads to a seizure or a semi-conscious state or a petit mal, or even only to a bad mood. They try to wake up—sleep epileptics into this world, waking epileptics into a higher world—and both fail. This is a constant and repeated experience leading from one disappointment to the next unless the seizures are interrupted, and unless measures of spiritual hygiene for adults and educational and curative measures for children are taken to counteract this continuously experienced fateful frustration.

We have seen that waking epilepsy can develop into sleep epilepsy and sleep epilepsy into diffuse epilepsy; this process is a degenerative one, weakening the personality. There is no way back out of diffuse epilepsy into sleep epilepsy or from sleep epilepsy to waking epilepsy. Seeing this will help us learn to understand what's really going on. The attempt at waking up is so seldom successful. It's condemned to failure again and again, and sleep epileptics go through the day as if they had heavy sacks over their heads. Children with absence seizures go through the day full of anxiety because any demand or challenge can bring on a loss of consciousness. Waking epileptics try again and again to raise themselves up above the level of day consciousness and sink back down again. It's all in vain. If we take this more and more into account, it becomes possible for us to acquire an overall image of this condition.

Let me remind you once again of what I tried to present yesterday, namely, that a kind of expansion or going-out takes place as we fall asleep, while in the moment or moments when we begin to wake up, a process of concentration, of narrowing down, of unification takes place. We can learn to perceive this if we practice just a bit of inner self-observation. We can notice how, when we fall asleep, part of our existence flows out through our hands and fingers, our legs, feet, and toes, how we proceed downward and outward away from our head, and then it gets dark. Then our possibility to consciously penetrate what happens to our soul is extinguished.

Spiritual research, however, can provide information about it. We can accept it or not, as we choose, but we are forced to admit that modern research into epilepsy shows us fundamentally and with astounding clarity the significance of the processes of waking and falling asleep. We don't need to debate the issue now. But we do need to point it out, and those wanting to inform themselves about it will find Rudolf Steiner's life's work at their disposal. It shows in many different ways what happens to us in the processes of waking and falling asleep. We are a duality when we sleep—one part, our bodily nature, remains lying in bed or wherever; the other part expands, breathes out, and lifts itself up, and only returns again in the morning.

Looking at it from the new point of view that every seizure is an attempt to wake up, let's return to what I presented when I said we must recognize human beings as threefold even in the structure of their consciousness. We have the head system where day-consciousness reigns, where we have concepts and thoughts and consciously recalled images. Next we have the middle system where the rhythmic processes of breathing and circulation are at work, and where we experience the content of our feelings in dream-consciousness. Finally we have the metabolic-limb system, where we are always asleep. I tried to explain that our consciousness here is sleep-consciousness, but it's still consciousness of a sort. This is the region where our will is at work.

Now, if someone wakes up in a seizure, this whole structure of consciousness is displaced one step upward, sleeping consciousness into the rhythmic system, dream-consciousness into the head area, and ordinary day consciousness out of the body altogether. This means that the physical organization, which together with the life-forces is what remains lying in bed when we sleep, is suddenly taken hold of by the soul's consciousness-structure in a totally different way than usual. This is no less real than anything I can see or touch. And what happens then? The will, instead of working in the muscles of the motor system and being guided by motives imposed on it by the human being, takes hold of the middle organization instead, and becomes subject only to the rhythms of the heart and lungs, resulting in a clonic-tonic convulsion. The muscular system, still sleeping, has become a part of the middle system. One step further up, feeling fills the head in the form of the aura. This aura is present not only before a seizure, but continues as long as it lasts; it is simply drowned out when total loss of consciousness sets in.

A person having a seizure lives in feeling (in the aura) in his or her upper system, experiencing tones, colors, and other sensations. The severe physical damage to nerve tissue caused by a seizure has to do with the fact that the brain is a kind of extraordinarily refined mirroring device that is only just adequate to reflect the light and darkness of thinking. If concepts enter that are saturated with sensation, with sympathy and antipathy, the brain breaks down under this repeated assault. Way up top, without any physical basis, thinking, which can otherwise possess consciousness and even self-consciousness due to the resistance offered by the head, flows out and drifts away, and unconsciousness takes its place.

The whole process of a seizure is one in which the personality, the ego of the human being, wakes up and tries to enter the body, but the epileptic constitution forcibly displaces consciousness upward, causing the seizure, and the lower part of the human being is suddenly left empty. Then the forces of nature stream into this lower human being, bringing destruction with them. Instead of standing, the person is seized by the forces of gravity and thrown to the ground. If you ever see an adult epileptic collapse in a grand mal or a child simply sink to the ground in a so-called akinetic petit mal, you'll notice how gravity takes hold of the body just as it usually takes hold of a stone falling to the ground. Water forces seize the person and the physical body swells up. Air streams in unhindered—not just the inhaled and exhaled air, but the forces of the air "inflate" the body. Warmth forces stream in and heat it up. The person's lower organization is invaded and destroyed by unimpeded forces of nature. This is the destruction we spoke about again and again.

You see, normally the ego resists these forces, coming to grips with gravity and buoyancy, air and water, so that we can be a Self. Otherwise we fall victim to nature-forces that stream in and destroy us. This is a comprehensive description of a convulsive seizure: Instead of walking, we fall; instead of doing, we convulse. Instead of clarity, there is unconsciousness; instead of cognition, there is destruction. That's what epilepsy is, and that was one of the subjects we wanted to cover.

As a counterimage to all this, I'd still like to discuss, if only briefly, what Rudolf Steiner describes as childhood hysteria. But before that I still want to point out something that has captured the attention of epilepsy researchers in recent years, something that will also help us understand hysteric forms of mental illness in childhood. They've found out that, after an extended course of drug therapy (which can be a brilliant success nowadays), something suddenly begins to happen that shows us the handwriting on the wall, as it were. The EEGs of a number of patients become totally harmonious, like those of normal people, in effect. But that's only the EEGs. The people themselves, once they're seizure-free or perhaps even *because they're seizure-free*, suddenly show symptoms that can scarcely be distinguished from acute psychosis.

In one of the latest studies, Tellenbach describes how he himself analyzed a group of patients in whom marked paranoid symptoms appeared after drug treatment normalized their electroencephalogram. It was possible to make the psychosis disappear by reducing the medication and recur by increasing it until the EEG became normal again. He concludes by saying, "We could not have been more surprised at the possibility of causing this alternation." Landolt, a leading epilepsy researcher in Zürich who was more or less the first to point out this phenomenon, puts it like this at the end of his study: "Today we are coming to the conclusion that there are limits to the treatment of epilepsy, in that the effect of some of the new anticonvulsants forces a choice on us—mental illness or epilepsy, insanity or seizures—and, of course, having seizures is still better than being mentally ill."[1]

Do you understand the gravity of a conclusion like that? It's really an extraordinary thing that we doctors are faced with the choice between epilepsy and psychosis. You can make people seizure-free, but if you do, you may find that they retreat mentally. We've actually known about this for thirty years, because that's how long we've been inducing epileptic seizures by means of electric or insulin shock in order to give schizophrenics the possibility to return to our world from theirs. Now we've acquired the opposite possibility through biochemical and pharmacological research, namely, the possibility of suppressing seizures at the expense of having psychosis set in.

Landolt is absolutely right to ask which is preferable. I believe there's only one answer to that—for epileptics, it's better to have seizures; for schizophrenics, it's better to have schizophrenia. We'll have to decide individually in each case, and we'll have to learn to recognize that we can't simply suppress something with some chemical and then believe the person is cured.

This is the cardinal problem that the treatment of epilepsy poses to the medical world: "If you decide to suppress seizures with drugs alone, you must be aware that the people may slip off into psychosis because their EEG becomes normal." The solution is to finally begin to educate epileptics to become strong enough to resist psychosis even when they're seizure-free. Then of course we can treat them with the usual drugs as well.

Having asked what a seizure really is, and having answered that it's an abortive waking process, we must now ask what psychosis is. It is an unsuccessful attempt at falling asleep, and in this process of falling asleep, people begin to have hallucinations, ideas we call "crazy," and so on. But just because those ideas are crazy, are they necessarily any less valid than the world of semblances surrounding the rest of us? This is a question we really need to ask nowadays.

Don't the mentally ill experience realities they can't master, realities that tear them apart and consume them? They are forced to defend themselves against these voices, these aspersions and temptations, because we in our normal daily life haven't taught them to be strong enough to face what's going on.

What I've told you here is only part of a sequence that began with mescaline and other drugs people took to send themselves off into a distorted spiritual world. Anticonvulsants can also do that to some people in a very similar way. If you don't get the dosages exactly right (which is exceedingly difficult because each individual taking them is new and different every day), you'll notice that these patients begin to suffer from loss of initiative, or semi-conscious states or difficulties in speaking. They either fall asleep totally or fall asleep to wake up in the spiritual world and go crazy because they can't withstand that kind of awakening. Only once we help them to establish a new relationship between their soul and spirit and their bodily nature and to experience that we ourselves will only be able to stand fast in the face of today's world if we take up a conscious path of self-education, concentration, meditation, and religious devotion, only once the spirit finally finds a place again in our view of ourselves as human beings, only then will we be able to say to epileptics, "Do these exercises three times a day to strengthen your thoughts, shed light on your feelings and illuminate your will" and give them the usual drugs in good conscience, knowing that they will be able to resist the temptations of psychosis in spite of being seizure-free.

Here we have a polarity between epilepsy and psychosis. And the forerunners of psychosis are the conditions Rudolf Steiner described as hysteric illness in children. Unlike epileptics, these children are not unable to wake up properly, but are rather, to use an expression of Steiner's, constantly in danger of "flowing out" and falling asleep. I'm sure each one of you will remember one or the other child like that as I describe them. These are children who may not be so terribly intellectually retarded to begin with, but who lose their intellectual capabilities more and more because of their environment's inability to meet their emotional needs.

They have an extraordinarily rich inner life, but are terribly vulnerable to the outer world. It's as if they were lacking a bit of covering or a piece of skin. If you speak to them too loudly, they withdraw; if you demand something of them, they get anxious. No seizures, nothing like that. But they begin to tremble. You'll notice that the sweat can literally drip from their armpits, palms, and fingers simply because they're constantly shrinking back from demands of daily life they can't live up to. If you really smell these children, you'll notice that they're often surrounded by a distinctive odor. What you should do with these children so they don't fall into psychosis later on is simply to approach their intentions with infinite delicacy. Never say directly, "Come on Anna, let's go for a walk now," or Anna will immediately start to sweat. But if you say to her, "Anna, in half an hour we're going to get ready to go for a walk," it will be a great relief for her not to have been addressed directly. If she doesn't have to suffer the pain of being called upon directly, then it's possible for this flowing-out to come to a halt. If you have children like this sit down in front of you and stroke them gently and say, "You can do it, you can do it," or if you sit beside them and do their assignment with them, it's comforting and healing. If you start gently changing the rhythm of reading or writing, beginning slowly and getting a little faster, slowing down again, getting faster, and carry it out step by step, and if you give these children forms to draw and imitate, then you'll counteract their inner tendency to fall asleep and fall apart.

What epileptics need is just the opposite. Epileptics—I'm speaking primarily about epileptic children and adolescents—need waking up and loosening up, need to be led step by step out of their constant dark mood of frustration.

Loosening them up through music-making and music appreciation and through painting with watercolors (which also has something musical in it) is what must be done for them. I've already spoken about adult epileptics. You see, waking and sleeping, waking up and falling asleep as universal human phenomena, weeping in waking up, laughing in falling asleep, concentration in the head, dissociation in the limbs—these are images we must begin to live with in order to humanize everything that's become inhuman and abstract nowadays, to the point where it's making our patients fall apart and forcing our children into abnormality.

It all depends on one thing—placing the spirit in the center of our existence again. In every form of occultism in the East and West, it's known that the year 1899 was a decisive point in human evolution, that in the year 1899 a five-thousand-year period described in Indian occultism, for instance, as Kali Yuga, the Dark Age, came to an end.

Humanity had to be cut off from the surrounding spiritual world during this dark age. During Kali Yuga, it was necessary for human beings to become citizens of the earth, to find their place in that tension between the sensory world of appearances and the destruction the forces of nature constantly subject us to from below. But this age is over. If you read Rudolf Steiner's descriptions of the beginning of this age around the end of the fourth millennium before Christ, then you'll realize that as soon as Kali Yuga began, what we now call epilepsy could also appear. Ever since then, epilepsy has been humankind's companion. Ever since then, a group of human beings has always been present to knock on the doors of awakening—on the doors of awakening into either this world or a higher world. They stand among us as reminders of the age of Kali Yuga. But now that this age is over, totally new spiritual insights into their condition become available, as indeed they must. To refer back to the quote by Vogel I read to you during the first lecture, it means that to the image of the epileptic boy portrayed by Raphael in his last painting, we must add the upper part of the picture showing the transfigured Christ. This is the crucial point, and as long as we don't really want to awaken to it in ourselves, we will continue to swing between seizures and psychosis, convulsions and insanity, and won't find any way out.

Notes

Three Ways of Diagnosing

1. J. Lutz, *Kinderpsychiatrie* ("Child Psychiatry"), Rotapfel-Verlag, Zürich & Stuttgart, 1964.

2. Max B. Clyne, *Night Call.*

Some Guiding Images in the Area of Motor Disturbances

1. J. Lutz, *Kinderpsychiatrie.*

2. Spastic paralysis is the most prevalent of these forms of so-called "brain paralysis".

Some Guiding Images in the Area of Sensory Disturbances

1. The curative-educational method of observation referred to here is less concerned with looking at separate functions that may be impaired than with trying to come to an understanding of what the sum total of abnormalities present actually means to the child in question. A similar paralysis may have a totally different impact on the life of a child if it is coupled with visual impairment instead of with a hearing deficit.

2. Here Karl König bases what he says on Rudolf Steiner's sensology, which in contrast to the usual conception distin-

guishes twelve human senses. The four mentioned here serve the purpose of perceiving one's own body.

3. Deliberately touching things is not what is meant here, but rather experiencing the boundaries of one's own body through repeated contact, through touch, with objects in the environment throughout the day.

4. Phenylketonuria is a congenital metabolic disorder.

5. The examples of blindness and deafness were chosen to make it clear to what an extent discriminating sense-perception, especially visual perception, is required in order to establish an appropriate distance from the rest of the world. Taking up contact with the world is only possible once this distance has been established. In blind and deaf children we can experience two archetypal disturbances of this process, so to speak. Of course, the effects of loss of vision or hearing can be mitigated to a great extent through the function of other senses, which step in as substitutes. Many contact-disturbed children, on the other hand, lack actively discriminating sensory perception as we've just described it, in spite of the fact that their vision is intact.

6. It's not for nothing that we use the word "grasp" figuratively to mean "understand." This example shows how an autistic child's bodily senses spread out into the immediate surroundings, which then, for lack of distance, are experienced as being part of his or her own body.

The Problem of Right and Left

1. In presenting the sound "ee" in eurythmy and curative eurythmy, Rudolf Steiner relates it especially to the experience of the ego.

2. Johann Wolfgang von Goethe, 1749–1832, German poet.

Famous particularly for his verse drama *Faust*. Also wrote extensively on botany, optics, and other scientific topics. Published his autobiography under the title *Poetry and Truth* (1811–1822).

Joseph Freiherr von Eichendorff, 1788–1857, German poet, novelist, and critic of the Romantic period. He published *Ahnung und Gegenwart* ("Presentiment and Present"), a prose work, in 1815.

3. See "Some Guiding Images in the Area of Sensory Disturbances," pp. 31–43 in this volume.

4. The numbers vary considerably from one researcher to another due to different methods of investigation and different population groups surveyed. They seem to agree that the number of left-handed people is increasing, but it's debatable whether this is a legitimate increase or the result of increasing tolerance of left-handedness. (J. Kramer, *Linkshändigkeit*, 1961, p. 24). We can assume a corresponding increase in the number of ambidextrous people.

5. The view presented in this paragraph has been superseded by more recent research. A summary of this research and recommendations for parents and teachers on dealing with left-handed children can be found in *Kindersprechstunde* by Dr. Michaela Glöckler and Dr. Wolfgang Goebel (Stuttgart: Urachhaus, 1988). A section from the relevant chapter is translated below:

> It is a basic fact in anatomy that the large nerve tracts supplying the big skeletal muscles cross in the medulla oblongata. Consequently, the cortex areas belonging to the nerves of the right side of the body are located in the left cerebral hemisphere. Correspondingly, the ones connected to the nerves on the left side are found in the right cerebral hemisphere. A "restructuring" would be possible only if one were to try to change the predominance of one side through comprehensive training by

doing other activities besides writing with the right hand. However, writing is an activity that is newly learned when children start school. Thus, it is misleading to speak of a "switch," for children have usually not yet learned to write when they start school. It is also wrong to believe that the speech center develops in the cerebral hemisphere connected to the dominant hand, and that therefore training children to write with the right hand could impair the speech center. Various tests (also on people recovering from brain surgery) have shown that in about 98% of all people (including the left-handed) the speech center is located in the left cerebral hemisphere. Thus, the development of the speech center is evidently independent of what hand we are writing with and what side of the body is dominant.

...

Rudolf Steiner described the development of a more or less pronounced left-handedness as the result of a previous incarnation and explained that the individual in question had overextended him or herself in body and soul in the preceding life. This resulted in a weakness of the right side, which lets the left side appear stronger and more dominant.

From this point of view, the predominance of the qualities of the left side appears as an opportunity for the individual to develop more inwardness and clarity of consciousness in the current incarnation. It is the task of educators, then, to support this intrinsic developmental potential and to avoid a weakening of the forces of the left side. However, this weakening is exactly what happens when the left hand is used throughout life for an activity that runs its course largely unconsciously after the complicated process of learning to write is completed and that serves primarily our communication with the outer world.

Thus, when a left-handed child learns to write with the right hand, the left side is relieved of an activity in which our consciousness normally does not follow the formation of each letter with interest, but instead is concerned with the content we write about. When we write with the right hand, then the right side will be given over entirely to an activity to which it is predisposed, namely to an activity oriented toward reality and practical life.

Since Waldorf pedagogy takes into account the results of Rudolf Steiner's spiritual scientific research, it is understandable that Waldorf teachers recommend that parents let their children learn to write with the right hand.

(From: Michaela Glöckler and Wolfgang Goebel, *Kindersprechstunde: ein medizinisch-pädagogischer Ratgeber*, 7th revised and expanded edition, Stuttgart: Urachhaus, 1988, pp. 438-439 and pp. 442-443.)

The World of Language

1. See "The Problem of Right and Left," pp. 45–58 in this volume.

2. H. Asperger, *Heilpädagogik*, 3rd ed., Vienna 1961, p. 237.

3. Ludwig Josef Johan Wittgenstein, 1889–1951, British philosopher, born in Vienna, died in Cambridge. Had great influence on logical positivism, linguistic analysis, and semantics.

The *Gestalt* of the Child

1. Karl König described the basic female constitutional types in 1962 at a conference for co-workers in the Camphill villages. See also *In Need of Special Understanding*, pp. 55ff, Camphill Press, 1986.

2. The "first growth spurt" (Zeller) when the small child's large-headed, short-limbed physique is transformed into the significantly more harmonious build of the schoolchild.

3. Karl König goes into more detail on this point in his book *Der Mongolismus* ("Mongolism"), 2nd ed., Stuttgart, 1969.

4. See "Some Guiding Images in the Area of Sensory Disturbances," pp. 31–43 in this volume.

An Introduction to Convulsive Disorders

1. P. Vogel, "Von der Selbstwahrnehmung der Epilepsie" ("Epilepsy as the Patient Sees It") in *Der Nervenarzt*, vol. 32 (1961), p. 438.

2. Rudolf Steiner, *Anthroposophy: An Introduction*, No. 234 in the Collected Works, (London: Rudolf Steiner Press, 1983).

Different Types of Convulsive Disorders

1. See Walter Holtzapfel, "Threefoldness in Petit Mal Seizures" in *Beiträge zu einer Erweiterung der Heilkunst*, vol. 12, no. 2, p. 60.

2. See D. Jantz, *Die Epilepsien*, ("Types of Epilepsy"), Stuttgart, 1969.

3. W. Zeller, *Konstitution und Entwicklung*, ("Constitution and Development"), Göttingen, 1964.

Epilepsy and Hysteria

1. H. Landolt in *Deutsche Zeitschrift für Nervenheilkunde*, 185, 411–430 (1963).